WE ARE ALL BROTHERS

WE ARE ALL BROTHERS

Louis Evely

Translated by
Sister Mary Agnes, O.P.

HERDER AND HERDER

1967
HERDER AND HERDER NEW YORK
232 Madison Avenue, New York 10016

Original edition: *Fraternité et évangile,*
published in 1963 by the author.

Nihil obstat: Brendan W. Lawlor, Censor Librorum
Imprimatur: ✠ Robert F. Joyce, Bishop of Burlington
September 26, 1966

WE ARE ALL BROTHERS

I.

"He who is of God, hears the words of God. The reason why you do not hear them is that you are not of God." (Jn. 8, 47)

And what about ourselves? Do we hear the word of God? Does the word of God speak to us? Does it tell us anything? Does it reveal anything? Is it for us a means of salvation? "Say but the word."

Between God and man a trial is ever taking place in which each one plays his part.

Man says, "God says nothing. God is far away, silent, indifferent, —a stranger. I call upon Him, I am a man of good will, and all I ask is that I may establish good relations between us. He is the One who encloses Himself in impenetrable silence. He is the One who condemns me to a monologue every time that I try to speak to Him."

And God replies that He is the Word. Revelation. Love. He says that He reveals Himself by love and that He has never ceased to love us nor to speak to us. God says that the hunger that man has for God is as nothing in comparison with the hunger that God has for man. Man can do without God, he may even come to the point where he believes that he is entirely self-sufficient, but God cannot do without man. God loves man. God needs man. A son or a daughter can behave quite independently and ignore father or mother, but no parent will ever behave that way towards his child.

"And even if a mother should forget her infant, I will not forget you," God tells us. "Look, I have graven thee upon the palm of my hand, thou art ever before my eyes."

Pascal says something charming: "You would not now be seeking me if you had not already found me." Perhaps it could be better said, "You would not now be seeking me if I had not found you." It is God who is seeking man, it is God who calls upon man and is not heard. The appeals of man to God are, in reality, responses, —responses to the appeals of God to man.

God is constantly revealing Himself. From the very dawn of history, God has been speaking of Himself to man.

In Paradise, God came to speak familiarly with Adam in the cool of the evening. In Paradise, God began to confide in man, to give Himself. And when someone confides in you, you have the power to betray his confidence. And Adam did just that. In Paradise, the Passion was begun. And also Calvary. And also the revelation of the infinite love of God for man.

Adam rejected God. He broke off his communication with Him, and darkness followed immediately. Both you and I know that darkness, a darkness in which God is no longer present to us, no longer speaks to us, but leaves us to ourselves. "Blessed are the clean of heart, for they shall see God!" This is a darkness which not only refuses the light but also fears it.

We know this state of things so well. It so often happens that the word of God is meaningless to us. And this is no indication that God is far from us, but rather that we are far from God.

After his sin, Adam hid himself behind a curtain of leaves. He did so in order that he might not hear God speak. And, as always, it was God who broke the silence, God who was the first to speak. "Adam, where are you? What are you doing down there? . . . Don't stay so far away. I came to talk to you. It is sad to be left all alone! Don't pretend that you do not hear me. Don't hide yourself, nor cover your ears. You know that I will call to you so tenderly, so lovingly, that you will be obliged to come to me. Do not hold back now. Come at once!"

And God acted this same way with Abraham. To Moses, He spoke face to face, as a man is wont to speak with his friend. He spoke by the prophets. And thus, on down to the day when the Word was made flesh and dwelt amongst us. He now dwells amongst us by His words, His Gospel. He is there in His entirety so that we may always listen to Him.

He is ever speaking. He has no more ceased to reveal Himself, than He has ceased to love. We all are aware of this; —when anyone is in love, everybody can see it. It speaks for itself. It cannot help manifesting itself. The mere fact that

11

God speaks to me is, in itself, a revelation of the truth that He wishes to make known. If He speaks to me, it is because He loves me. As He never ceases to love, so He never ceases to speak. And He speaks to you.

But man has always been dissatisfied with the revelation made by God. It is a matter of history. We ought to see our own selves in this dissatisfaction because it is our surest means of avoiding it.

God spoke to Adam by means of every created thing, —by every tree. Adam learned that one tree was missing and he became dissatisfied. He wanted some other form of communication, some other revelation, another tree!

God conducted the Hebrews through the desert by a path strewn with marvels. Miracles were multiplied at every step. And yet they murmured. "Oh, that manna! So monotonous! Always the same! We remember the onions that we used to eat every day in Egypt as we sat beside the pots of cooking meat and ate as much as we wanted. And the cucumbers! The leeks! The garlic! Here we see nothing but that manna. You have led us into the desert so that we may die of hunger."

And it is the same with us. Our own dissatisfaction with the word of God, has already been prophesied. Like the Hebrews of old, we also desire a spicier diet.

After Christ had come, so many people criticized the way in which He manifested Himself. His fellow citizens felt that He did not work enough miracles. His relatives told

Him, "Any person who claims to be what you claim to be should be more in public." Even His precursor ended by sending a small embassy to Him to ask, "Are you the one who is to come, or are we to look for someone else?" And at the foot of the cross, His enemies (and not a few of His friends) insulted Him by saying: "Come down from that Cross! Don't hang there motionless! Do something! Act! Come down triumphantly! With glory! Strike terror in these onlookers and they will all believe in you! Your revelation of yourself is such a miserable thing, so unsatisfying! Is this all we are going to get?"

And we ourselves are not satisfied with the way in which God reveals Himself to us. It seems to us that He does not speak at all.

*   *   *

There is a book which Christians do not read. There is a book which Catholics hardly ever read. There is a book— and I am not a prophet, but I will venture to predict that you will die without reading it, and that book is the Gospel.

Among all the books in my library, there is one which has never been borrowed. All my books are borrowed at some time or other, and sometimes they are even returned. Boys and girls come to my home, —they are young people of the free-and-easy modern type, —they look around my library, they take out a book here and there, they turn over a few pages, sometimes they even consult me. But there is one book which they never so much as lift off the shelf, and that book is the Gospel.

It is a book they are perfectly sure has no message for them, nothing of interest. So many other books attract them, so many other books intrigue them. A friend, a teacher, a passing acquaintance, perhaps, has recommended some particular book, and they undertake the reading of it. But the recommendation of Almighty God means nothing.

Do not be deceived by the number of Bibles that are actually bought. I can tell you where they are. They are on the shelf of some cupboard, untouched. And your own Bible, where is it?

Catholics do not nourish their souls with the word of God. God has sent them a letter and they put it in their pocket without even reading it. God has given them a "testament." Suppose your old parents had left you a "testament." You would certainly open it to see whether by chance, they had left you something. But, when it comes to God, you are so sure that He has not left you anything that you will not so much as look at the letter.

This is going to cause you a rather embarrassing entrance into heaven.

When you reach heaven and you see our Lord, overflowing with love and joy, so happy at your arrival, for the first time you will become your real self, you will be truly born again beneath the gaze of Him who alone knows you as you really are. He has called you and He loves you. Then you will exclaim, "Ah! If only I had known that you were like this! If only I had known you better! Why is it that no one told me about you? What were all those priests doing? How is it that they never said anything? My life would have been so different! I would have been happy all the time. I would have encouraged so many others. My life would have been consecrated to the witnessing of my faith and my joy at being loved like this."

Our Lord will reply, "How did it happen that you never knew? I know very well that the sermons of my priests are not always masterpieces, but I took care to leave behind a very faithful portrait of myself. Did you never read my Gospel?"

Then you are going to have a bad time of it for the next couple of minutes.

What if our Lord insists? "My poor child, was it because you had no time for reading? Were you so overworked? What were the books that you considered more necessary? More important? More interesting?"

How will you feel when you enumerate the titles?

But there is more to come.

At every Mass, the Gospel is read. Sometimes it is chanted, explained, commented upon; but however it is read, it is quickly forgotten.

Christ Himself told us that this is a proof of the existence of the devil. We have several proofs in our own daily lives that the devil exists. Not proofs imposed upon us by authority, but proofs from our own experience, and one of them is the really preternatural way in which we forget the word of God. At times, we hardly seem to hear it.

I make the following experiment time and time again whenever I preach a day of recollection or a retreat, and it never fails. Sometimes, it is right after the Sunday Mass; sometimes, the next day; sometimes, in the middle of the week. I ask, "What was the Gospel last Sunday?"

The minds of my listeners become a perfect blank. Does yours? The word of God has been announced, has been spoken to you. He has told you of His love. He has provided you with your rations for the coming week, your "viaticum," the word of God which should nourish and strengthen you. "Say but the word and my soul will be healed." And you have no sooner heard it than you have forgotten it, no sooner received it than you have lost it.

"Mary kept all these words," and we Christians hardly take the trouble to listen to them. They are no sooner said than they are forgotten.

Christ assures us that this is supernatural. He attributes it to the intervention of the devil. He sees Satan, like a crow, a sinister pilferer, hiding in a corner of the field. As soon as the good seed is sown, he flies over and steals it before it has a chance to grow.

It is not like this with the other books we read. If we read a novel, see a motion picture, a play, or something on television, we easily remember it. We can retell the whole story.

16

We can go over in our minds what we have read, or seen, and recapture the most interesting scenes, the ones that we enjoyed the most.

We are impressed by everything, everything leaves its mark upon us. It is only the word of God that leaves us unimpressed, leaves no impression, disappears without a trace, leaves us completely indifferent.

And yet, it is this same word of God which has created us. "God spoke, and light was made." Each of us has been called into existence by a word of God. Each of us is a word of the living God, intended for the edification of all the rest. Our vocations, our destinies, our conversions, our entry into religion, our presence at spiritual conferences, all these are due to a call from God, to a summons from the word of God. We came into existence only because God pronounced our name. Each time that He repeats it, we experience a new birth, our life brightens, our heart expands, our joy increases, and it seems to us that we are only now beginning to live.

The "People of God," the Church, came into being by a call, a word of God which assembled it, and this is why the word of God is—or should be—proclaimed at the beginning of each of our Christian assemblies. It is the word of God which has created and preserved the People of God.

It is also the word of God which will one day judge us. Are we aware of the fact that we have no other judge? "The Father judges no one." The Father is not a judge. He is a father. "The Father has given all judgment to the Son."

17

And the Son judges no one. "For I have not come to judge the world but to save it."

Neither the Father nor the Son will judge us. They are love, pity, pardon, mercy. They are not judges.

Who, then, is to judge us?

The word! We shall be judged by the word of God, in accordance with these words: "If anyone hears my sayings and does not keep them, I do not judge him; for I did not come to judge the world but to save the world. He who rejects Me and does not receive my sayings has a judge; the word which I have spoken will be his judge on the last day." (Jn. 12, 47–48)

The judgment will be based on these questions: "Has the word of God spoken to you? Has the word of God healed you? Has the word of God borne fruit in you? Are you one of those sheep who hear His voice and follow it?"

Or do you judge the word of God? "It means nothing to me." Very well. Accept its judgment of you in order that you may not be condemned by it on the last day: "The reason why you do not hear is that you are not of God."

It is also the word of God that will raise us up on that last day. "The hour is coming, and now is, when the dead will hear the voice of the Son of God, and those who hear will live." (Jn. 5, 25)

The word of God is able to raise even the dead! There exists in all of us the need for a resurrection, a zone of inertia calling for revival.

But, you will tell me, I have tried what you recommend. Long ago I bought a copy of the Gospels. I opened the book and tried to read it, but it was useless. It meant nothing to me. The story was so well known, the characters so lifeless, the country so distant, the sense so difficult! Oh yes, I read it through to the end, not because I wanted to read it but because I did not want to be told that I had not read it.

Why this sad failure?

Because you have not read it properly.

Before reading the word of God, the thing to do is to kneel down and pray. "Without me, you can do nothing." No one can understand the word of God all by himself. The Fathers of the Church tell us that the same grace is necessary to him who hears the prophecy and to him who utters it. The Spirit who inspired the writer must also inspire the reader. Every word of Scripture, if it is not to remain a dead letter, should be revitalized by that breath of the Spirit of God who reanimated the dried bones.

Furthermore, we should not "read" the word of God, but "listen" to it. This is a very different thing. In reading the Gospel, we handle a dead book, we exhume ancient history. In listening, we are attentive to a living voice, to words which are being pronounced at the present moment, which are addressed directly to us, which concern ourselves, which are aimed at us, which denounce us.

"For the word of God is living," St. Paul tells us. Have you discovered this? It is living, active, sharper than any two-edged sword, piercing, . . . even to discerning the thoughts and intentions of the heart. It has a great work to do in each one of us. Open your hearts so that it may act. Listen to it, for it speaks to you.

When you receive Holy Communion, you do not receive Christ who lived some two thousand years ago, but the Christ of the present day, alive now. When you open the book of the Gospels, you are not reading something that took place long ago, but something that applies here and now. Its message is for you—now.

Not only must we hear this word of God but we must meditate upon it. "Blessed are they who hear the word of God and keep it." To meditate means to go over it again and again until it speaks to you. And this takes time. Moreover, there are two ignorant ways of reacting to God's word, both equally stupid, which we must beware. The first is to exclaim, "This is magnificent! I understand everything! It is all so clear!" And the other is to say, "I don't understand a word of it. It is very discouraging. Let's close the book. It teaches me nothing." Between the two there is the only sensible attitude, that of the Blessed Virgin Mary. "She understood not what He said to them, but she kept all these things, repeating them in her heart." Do you know any better way to listen to the words of God than that of the Blessed Virgin? We are such strangers to God, all our spiritual senses are so inefficient, and all our religious perceptions are so nearly dead. Consequently we must pray, beseech, supplicate, and repeat again and again the same things in the depths of our hearts until the word of God speaks to us.

We all regret that, unlike ourselves, many Protestants do not venerate the Holy Eucharist. But, in these days of ecumenism, we Catholics should learn to imitate their cult of the word of God.

Let us learn to treat the Bible, the Gospel, as a sacred book, a communication from God, to hold it in our hands as if it were the Holy Eucharist. God is present in the sacred Host, and He speaks to us from the sacred books.

The Orthodox Greeks do not reserve the Blessed Sacrament on the altar. Instead, they enthrone the Book of the Gospels and surround it with lighted candles. And there is logic in this. You may not communicate more than once a day, but you can hear God's word as often as you wish. In the Gospels, He is always accessible. Man does not live by bread alone, not even the Eucharistic Bread, but by every word that comes from the mouth of God.

Treat the Bible with the same respect that you would treat the Eucharist. You would be horrified if you saw a consecrated Host neglected, thrown on the ground, lost, but how do you treat the words of life?

For instance, suppose you came upon a consecrated Host and did not know that it was consecrated. For you, it was like ordinary bread. Suppose a little altar boy wanted to know what the altar bread tasted like and he ate, unknowingly, a consecrated Host. This would not be a sacrilege. He did not know that it was consecrated. But neither would he be receiving Communion. Not a single grace would he receive. He thought it was ordinary bread and, for him, that is what it was.

And so, if you read the Gospels as you would read an ordinary book, without reverence, without faith, it is for you an ordinary book. It will have no effect upon your spiritual life. No grace will come to you.

Even in the case of Christ Himself, all those who came to Him without faith, all those who regarded Him as an ordinary man, to them He was an ordinary man. He gave them none of His graces, He could not work a miracle.

Recall that sick woman in the crowd who wanted to get near to Him, saying, "If I but touch the fringe of His mantle, I shall be cured." The crowd was packed so densely around Him that approach was impossible. Then, suddenly there was a backward movement in the crowd and she found herself able to touch Him. Immediately she felt a great sense of health and well-being. She was cured! And at the same moment, Christ stood still. "Who has touched me?" He demanded. The apostles, realists as always, replied, "How do we know?" "Everyone is touching you!" "We are so jostled by this crowd! If only they would keep at a little distance!" But Christ ignored them. "Some one touched me," He repeated, "for virtue has gone out from me."

Then it began to dawn upon them that something serious

had taken place. Each one drew back, each one sought to excuse himself, each one tried to defend himself. "Me? I did nothing." "Me? I did not touch you." "Me? I was not even there!" And the poor woman stood alone in the middle of the circle and acknowledged what she had done. "I was the one who touched you."

Christ looked upon her and said, "Your faith has saved you. Go in peace!"

Notice: everyone touched Him. Everyone jostled against Him. But not one of them was cured. Only one touched Him with respect and with faith and with love. She was transformed, healed, and made whole.

It is the same with the Gospels. Everyone handles it, skims through the pages in a superficial way, and not one of them finds any spiritual nourishment in it, not one of them is changed, not one of them has made an act of faith.

What is the meaning of "to read with faith"?

To look upon the Gospel as the record of happenings some two thousand years ago is to treat it as a book of history, and to attach no more importance to it than to any other serious book of history.

The Gospels are much more than history, —they are a prophecy, a revelation. The Gospel shows us what is happening now and what will continue until the end of time. It is a light by which to direct our own life and every other life as well. It enables you to see that, for you, too, the Word was made flesh and still dwells among us.

The Gospel is God dwelling among men. God dwells ever among men. "I am with you always." And God is ever the same, —loving, patient, discreet, never imposing Himself upon us. He offers Himself, He whispers, He calls, He speaks. And it is so easy to pretend that we do not hear Him. It is so easy to reduce God to silence!

Mankind is ever the same, gross, negligent, distracted, thick of skin, and hard of hearing. He reproaches God for being silent, and, at the same time, is too careless to listen to Him.

The Gospel reveals to us what is ever happening, —how God acts towards us and how we act towards Him; how He treats us and how we treat Him, —or rather, mistreat Him.

The Gospel foresees, foretells, and denounces us. Open the Gospel and see yourself. Learn how you are spending your time. "Forgive them, for they know not what they do."

We know not what we do, but we can know and we should know, for we have a Revelation. Let the Gospel reveal us to ourselves. It is only when we see ourselves in the Gospel that the book will begin to speak to us.

The Gospel is a mirror. You know very well what a mirror is for. You look into it.

But, strange to say, no one does that with the Gospel. We look into it and see, not ourselves, but others! We become indignant at the incredulity of the Jews. "Just think! God spoke to them and they would not listen to Him! Christ was in their midst and they did not recognize Him! How was it possible to be so indifferent and hard!"

When one of the early kings of France first heard the story of the Passion of our Lord, he shed tears and exclaimed, "If I had been there with my army, things would have turned out very differently." And all the while, he was doing far worse than anything the Jews had done. He had pillaged cities, massacred the people, despoiled the widow and the orphan, but, when the mirror of the Gospel was held up to him that he might see himself therein, that he might compare it with his own behavior, he saw only other people and was scandalized.

Do we not act just as he did?

Let us make a little experiment. You all know the parable of the sower and the seed. Christ tells us that, if the word of God has not yet made a great change in us, it is not the fault of the seed. Nor is it the fault of the sower, —the preacher. Everything depends upon the soil upon which the seed falls.

So then, instead of making our habitual examination of the conscience of the preacher (was he too long?, more tiresome than usual?, did he contradict himself?, and so on), let us, for once, examine the conscience of the hearers and let us ask why it is that the word of God is so unfruitful in us.

There are four kinds of hearers, four kinds of soil on which the word falls.

First, there is the highway, —hardened, impenetrable, macadamized by habits. The seed falls there and remains on the surface. These hearers have heard so many sermons, and

25

none of them has effected the least change. They expect nothing and they acquire nothing. They are without any hunger for the word of God. Who is there among you who is so poor that he has come here in search of that light and that food which he needs to maintain his spiritual life? Who has faith enough to believe that God, who spoke to Moses through the burning bush, can also speak to his own soul through no matter what preacher? Those who are symbolized by the highway certainly have not this faith. When the sermon begins, they immediately fall asleep, or they take up again their favorite dreams, their accustomed concerns, their interests, their plans for the future. If the thoughts with which some people occupy themselves during the time that God is trying to touch their hearts were to be revealed, most of us would be shocked.

The second class is that of the superficial. These are sentimental enthusiasts, all on the surface. They do not know themselves, and are completely ignorant of the fact that their bad habits, their egotism, their inconstancy, their pride offer great opposition to the word of God. They have never tried to remove these stones which impede the growth of the good seed. They take offense easily and yet they believe themselves to be thoroughly converted because their emotions are stirred. If it should happen that they shed a few tears, they regard this as a sign of much virtue. Everything they hear touches them but leaves not the least mark. They hasten to repeat to others the thoughts that they heard in the sermon, and never let them take root in their own souls. They praise the preacher to the skies, but, because they are so self-satisfied and so pleased with having discovered, listened to, and given their approval of the preacher, they dispense themselves from all further effort in the acquisition of virtue.

The third class is the good, rich soil in which the word of God can take root. These are the people of mature mind, given to reflection. But they hasten to choke the growth of the seed for fear that it might take hold of them and lead them too far. They are occupied with their work and find their present life so well filled that they feel that they have a right to neglect their eternal life. They are taken up with too many things to have time to give to God. They are too intelligent to bow to the simplicity of the evangelist. They always find some objection to make, some reason to contradict, some mistake to laugh at, some good excuse for dropping the whole subject. Even while they are listening, they are fighting a mental tilt with the preacher and vanquishing him.

These are the worst of all. Deliberately closed to the word of God. Letting the thorns of their pride, their occupations, their mockery, grow on purpose in order to stifle the growth of the good grain which they regard as a menace.

And finally, where is that good soil which receives the seed with gratitude and lets it come to fruition? Where is the field in which the word of God bears fruit? I am not afraid to tell you that the ones among you who have recognized themselves in the first three categories, are that soil.

They are those who see themselves in the mirror of the

word of God, recognize themselves. "That one is myself. He is speaking about me." They take it to themselves, open their hearts and give the seed a chance to grow. They accept criticism and give up that good opinion of themselves and receive this revelation that God makes to them. They allow themselves to be judged by the word of God in order that they may not be condemned by it on the last day.

Then does the seed germinate, gow, ripen, and bring forth magnificent fruit.

The word of God is not only a revelation, but it also acts. It illumines and it also transforms. I believe in the sacramental efficacy of the word of God. Every Sunday we solemnly assemble to assist at the efficacy of a single word of God. The true Gospel of the Mass is not that which is read after the epistle. That one is a preparation, an introduction to the central mystery. The true Gospel of the Mass is the consecration.

What is the consecration? It is but a passage of the Gospel, read with faith, heard with faith, resuming the efficacy with which it was pronounced the first time. It is filled anew with the power, the inspiration of the Spirit of God, and accomplishes what it signifies.

A word, and the bread is transformed, transubstantiated! And before each Communion, we kneel and say—mechanically?, or sincerely?—"Lord, say but the word and my soul will be healed."

Is this true? Has He ever said a word? Have you ever

heard a word that benefited you? That healed you? This is a serious question to ask, but we must submit to the judgment of ourselves by the word of God in order to avoid being one day condemned by it. Each one of you has in his possession this book filled with such words. What are you waiting for? Go and put your faith to the test; if not, then go and act out your duplicity where you will, but not in the chapel, and certainly not at the communion rail.

Mary lived out her life with some words of God which she kept ever in her heart. And you, what are your provisions for life's journey? Have you, in your heart, a selection of the words of God which nourish you, strengthen you, and console you? What are these words which mean so much to you?

"Say but a word!" The priest pronounces some words over the bread and it is so docile, so completely at the disposal of God, that it is transformed.

And over ourselves, how many words? They slide off, merely graze the surface, and are lost. What must be our resistance to God, our hostility, our indifference, that we can remain so utterly unmoved by Him!

It is a shame to say it, but it is true nevertheless, that the greater number of Christians are such because of tradition, or force of habit. They are Christians for family reasons, or out of routine. In the time of Christ, they would have been among His persecutors. They do not really believe in God, but only in those who have spoken about Him. They have the outward appearance of Christianity, but, inwardly, there is a great void. They have had no personal experience of God. God has never spoken to them.

Think of it! At the time of Christ, people were converted just by listening to Him.

Suppose one day the Chief of Police in Jerusalem decided to arrest Jesus. His men were sent out to take Him prisoner.

Jesus was in the Temple, addressing a large crowd. Perhaps, for the sake of prudence, to avoid an uproar, or perhaps out of curiosity, since they were simple fellows, the policemen stayed in the back, putting off the arrest until the end of the discourse, and meanwhile listening to Him.

The seed of the word of God was scattered in their direction, too. It entered their hearts, penetrating to the depths. After a while they looked at each other, still listening, and then they did not dare to look at one another. When Jesus stopped speaking, they turned on their heels and went back to the police station.

The Chief of Police questioned them. "What happened? You did not see Him?" — "Oh yes, we saw Him." — "And you did not arrest Him? Was there some trouble? Did the crowd get in the way?" — "Not at all." — "Then what?" — "We couldn't do it. No one has ever spoken to us like this man has."

They were simple fellows, not intellectuals, not given to pleasure. "Father, I give you thanks that you have hidden these things from the wise and prudent, and have revealed them to little ones," —these policemen.

They had risked their promotion, their career, perhaps their liberty and their life as well, all because of the impression made upon them by the word of God.

And we, with our Christian heritage, have we ever recognized Christ with the ardor and the generosity of these simple folk? Can we testify that "no one has ever spoken to us like this man has?" If not, then what testimony can we give regarding Him?

How did they recognize Christ? Why were they converted to Him? How does one come into personal contact with Him?

By listening to Him with an open mind, in a spirit of receptivity, of acceptance, of docility, such as one finds in the poor.

At the approach of the Creator, the creature experiences strong emotions. Those who are of God are ravished with delight when they hear His words. His sheep hear and recognize His voice and they begin to move. His words meet their needs so well that they are unable to say whether they come from within themselves or from without. They stir the deepest regions of their souls. They know God and they know themselves, —it seems as if it were for the first time. Never have they known themselves to be so weak, so sinful, so blind, so deaf, so unworthy of God. But neither have they ever felt God so near, so tender, so merciful, and so good. Never before have they been so happy and never before have they suffered so much. Their hearts burn within them, as He speaks to them and explains the Scriptures. An im-

31

mense outburst of faith, of love, and of confusion springs up within their souls. God is understood, God is revealed, God has spoken to the soul. And with that marvelous revelation, the heart is quieted, nourished, and transformed. The blind see, the deaf hear, the lame walk, the sick are healed, and the dead come back to life.

When such as these return to their homes, so completely changed as to be hardly recognizable, the rest of the family begin to ask, "What has happened to you? Why are you like this? What did He say to you? What proofs did He give? What is so extraordinary about Him?"

They find that they are unable to explain, and they keep silence in order not to lose the memory of it all, in order to remain in that state of near ecstasy in which His words have placed them. And they conclude by saying, "No one has ever spoken to us like this man has."

Shame on that religion which has no witnesses save those of times past. What we need is witnesses of the present. Has Christ ever spoken to you as no one else can?

Bear in mind that, if you wish to become a person whose Christianity is contagious, you will have to become a Christian who is completely filled with God, nourished by Him, healed by Him, bearing the impress of contact with Him.

You will not be an adult, a "grown-up," in your religion, capable of exercising an apostolate, until you can say to those who instructed you in your religion what the men of Samaria said to the woman: "We no longer believe because of what you have said, for we have heard Him ourselves. We know that He is the Saviour of the world."

So with ourselves. We shall never be really converted, never have any enthusiasm for our religion, until we can say to our parents, our priests, our teachers, "Now it is not only because of what you have taught us that we believe, but because we ourselves have heard Him. He Himself has spoken to us, His words are my spiritual food, they have healed me, reanimated my courage, brought me back to life when I was not aware of being dead, and now I know that He is the Saviour of the world!"

When I was young I used to think that Jesus Christ had saved the world two thousand years ago. Now that I have had the opportunity to meet people and to receive their confidences, I know that the word of God is acting in the world now, today, at the present time. I know that there is a saving force at work in the world, and that it can affect us, and that we, too, can be cured. Prove it. Try it. Offer yourself to it, open your heart and ask it to speak to you. Ask that it transform you, and give back to you life and joy.

Then will you be witnesses, apostles. You will be able to go to others and invite them to share your experiences. It will no longer be necessary to be born a Catholic in order to believe, it will be sufficient to take up the Bible and listen to the word. Let Him say but one word and many will testify that no one has ever spoken to them like this man has.

Let us conclude with a prayer. Let us ask the Blessed Virgin to open our hearts to the word of God.

Mary is the one who first listened to the word, who was so filled with it that the Word of God became flesh and she gave Him to the world.

Each of us has the same office, the same destiny as Mary.

In each one of us the word of God should become a living thing. Each one of us, in the midst of our family, in our home, in our neighborhood, should make God something vital, should give God to the world.

Let us ask Mary that, in each of us, the Word of God may become flesh and be made known to the world.

II.

A CERTAIN number of ways have been suggested for beginning the reading of the Gospels. The first, it is quite evident, is to consider it as something that is actual, addressed directly to ourselves and concerned with ourselves. Thus we read and listen to such words as those St. John the Baptist addressed to the people of his day when he announced to them the presence of Christ who had been living among them for some thirty years: "There is one in the midst of you whom you know not." Or those which Christ used when, after three years of intimacy, of confidence and of miracles, He reproached His apostles for their stupidity and hardness of heart: "So long a time have I been with you and you do not yet know me!" And I think that each of us feels that He saw us at that time, too.

Any reading of the Gospel, either with or without method or commentary, is useful if done with an open mind. But there are helps and instructions which we can employ with profit.

This is the method which one family has followed. Each Sunday a text is chosen from the Gospel. The father of the family consults a commentary so as to be sure of the sense of the passage, and then, during the week which follows, father, mother, and the children read and think over this same text. On the following Sunday, they come together and each one tells, very simply, what that text has meant to him.

After the first six months, their religious life was transformed. They came to know why they are Christians. Their daily lives and their conversations have now taken their inspiration from the Gospel. They have come to realize what life can be when lived according to the Gospel.

Following this idea, I should like to point out an indispensable condition for the profitable reading of the Gospel, and that is poverty.

The main reason why God does not speak to us, or rather, why we do not hear God speaking to us, is told us by the Gospel itself: we are rich.

I do not refer to money, to what you may have in your pocket, but to your wealth of prejudices, set habits, laziness, torpidity. We provide for ourselves so that we have no need of God. We are quite sufficient for ourselves, our knowledge of religion is adequate, and our religious practices are all that they should be.

Every time that I have been asked an interesting question regarding religion, it has come from a non-believer. Catholics have no questions to ask. They feel certain that they know all about it. They have swallowed their religion with the salt of their baptism, and, for the rest, they are not interested enough to ask any questions. They have no desire to know or to do anything more.

We have instances of persons having been converted by simply reading the Gospel. They were without any faith before that. Whenever I see a copy of the Gospel in someone's hands, I know at once that he is either a recent convert or an unbeliever. Catholics are inoculated.

Another thing which prevents us from understanding the word of God is the fact that we do not expect to receive anything from God. There is no greater, no more unforgivable sin than to expect nothing from God. People will tell you, "I am too old (and they say this at sixteen as well as at sixty), I cannot change now. I have often tried and have always failed. It is too late!"

Faith means to believe that God has something to say to us. The real atheist is not one who says that God does not exist (which God? The one that so many Christians have disfigured and deformed? I agree with him!), but the one (and he exists, even among you, as I know because of many examples) who says that God will never change him, that God cannot effect any transformation in his life.

God is in search of people who expect Him to give them everything, people who really believe that "with God, nothing is impossible." In a word, people who are really poor.

The poor man is magnanimous. His hope in God is boundless. He firmly believes in the great things that God can do, and will do, for the poor.

Only a poor man can really understand God, for he is freed from himself. He allows himself to be criticized, to be set aside, to be pushed into action by the word of God. "You are clean [this means "poor"] because of what I have said to you."

The word of God can make a person very poor. To revise one's life and bring it into accordance with the teaching of the Gospel can give rise to some uncomfortable questions on the part of others. "My sheep hear my voice and they follow me."

A rich person is settled. He can make use even of the word of God to stay where he is, to justify his refusal to make any change. "Father, I give you thanks that you have hidden these things from the wise and prudent [that is, the rich], and revealed them to little ones," —the poor, those who take to themselves the word of God.

The starting point of the Christian life is poverty. It is the port of entry into the Kingdom, the Kingdom which belongs to the poor.

Are you one of these poor? Do you want more and more of wealth, or more and more of poverty? Do you want God to increase your wealth or would you prefer that He teach you how to despoil yourself of what you have? Disagreeable questions, these, but necessary preliminaries which have discouraged not a few, "for they had great riches."

What is poverty?

First of all, it is not a question of economics. To be without money is not a virtue. Too many people, as soon as there is question of poverty, begin to consult their checkbook. As soon as anyone tries to lift himself out of the rut of Christian mediocrity, the question of poverty arises. This is good, but he usually tries to solve this problem in too material a fashion. Where does poverty begin? What kind of furniture does a poor person have? And what about that insoluble problem of poverty in dress?

Then, perhaps, he sells his expensive car and buys a much cheaper make. Heroic act, but after that it too often happens that he begins to feel contempt for his friends who continue to ride comfortably in their own expensive cars and, while still calling themselves good Christians, do nothing to follow his good example.

Attention, everyone! That poverty which is acquired is a contradiction in terms. Do not expect to receive a decoration for your poverty! "Lord, I give you thanks that I am poor" is the prayer of the Pharisee. An ancient Greek called out to his friend, "Antisthene, I can see your pride through the holes in your cloak!"

Undoubtedly, there is a double menace here. A double hypocrisy. On the one hand, we may regard poverty as being solely a spiritual matter. "I am poor in spirit! So I keep everything!" This is a painless poverty. Take a few bills out of your pocketbook now and then in order to make sure that, as the surgeons say, you have no "adhesions."

On the other hand, we may come to think that poverty is entirely a matter of material possessions. Get rid of everything and then be in peace. Far from it! You will never become poor so easily as all that. You will never be poor at one stroke and once for all. It takes a lifetime to become poor. Above all, you will never become poor as long as you can give an account of it to yourself. Poverty, like humility, is one of those virtues that, when you think you have it, you can be sure you do not.

The first requirement in regard to poverty is poverty of spirit. We are all called to that, no matter the size of our bank account. This kind of poverty means that we understand our human limitations and have given up the ambition to be sufficient unto ourselves, and that we turn to God in our needs, with hope and with confidence.

Every man is a poor man, and he seldom realizes it. Poverty in the economic sense can be a real blessing because it is a revelation, a sensible sign, a sacrament of our great and universal poverty, —our poverty of soul, our lack of faith and of love. Happy, I say, are they who know real hunger and thirst. By this they know, and by this they tell the world that there is rottenness in the kingdom of this world, that the world is in need of transformation.

Suffering and sickness are also forms of poverty, and they render a like service to the world.

In the Gospel there seems to be something of a privilege given to material poverty and physical suffering. Why? Are not the sufferings of the mind far more painful than those of the body? And is not spiritual poverty far worse than lack of money?

Yes, but these moral miseries can always be hidden, de-

nied, dissimulated, forgotten. Happy are they who are un-
deniably poor. Happy are they whose suffering is visible.
They are irrefutable witnesses to mankind of our human
misery and our need for God.

But poverty and suffering are far from making us better.
While they do not always bring us to the virtue, they do
bring us to the truth. They teach us about ourselves. Man is
fundamentally poor, and if he is not so materially, he can
be desperately poor morally. Material poverty and physical
suffering are but signs, revelations, warnings of our profound spiritual indigence.

Those of us who are sick have no monopoly on misery. All
mankind is sick and poor and is so ignorant of it. It is our
mission to show that it is possible to accept poverty and sickness and at the same time to be happy.

But know well that if you are happy and rich, that is, if
you are happy because you are rich and all goes well with
you, you do not portray God to the world.

And if you are a discontented poor person, unhappy because you are poor, you can teach me nothing. I am just like
you.

But, if you are a happy poor person, a happy sick person,
a happy unhappy person, then you astonish me, you are as a
torch-bearer, showing God to men who are in search of Him.

For you have found One who is great enough to bear with
you your humiliation, One strong enough to support your
frailty, One good enough to relieve your unhappiness, lov-

ing enough to comfort your solitude, and render you a beacon to others.

Each of us ought to stand up and tell the rest what has been his own experience of human misery, how he has learned that he is not an exception, isolated, crushed. Rather, how he has become a brother to all who suffer, a companion to all in misery, how his experience has made it possible for him to enter into the fraternity of all humanity, to encourage and comfort those who cannot, or will not, accept their own poverty or misfortune.

Wealth blinds, wealth isolates. Poverty alone is fraternal. Only the poor man is an apostle. And this is the apostolic mission which lies open to our sick and suffering brethren.

But, to go back, how and when did you learn that every man is poor?

As for myself, I learned this when I was very young. I recall all the families with which we used to associate, especially during our vacations, either at the seaside or in the mountains. I do not know whether you have had this same experience, but, in my case, every time I became acquainted with a family and visited them in their home, I used to think that they were much better off than we were. They seemed so happy and such a united family. I admired the father, I loved the mother, and was enchanted with the children. And, often, —no, always—, at the very time when I was most in admiration of them, telling my friend, "What good luck you have! Your father is so good and wise, your mother so bright and gay and gentle! How happy you must be!", then I would learn that in that very family there was some sorrow, some misfortune, some disgrace. The veil was torn aside, and I was amazed. I would go back to my own home, thinking, "Those poor people! How much better off we are! We are the ones who are the most fortunate!"

I do not mean that we should be suspicious of others, that we should try to pry into their affairs, to try to guess what their troubles might be, because this is something that we do not know. On the contrary, we should always look upon others as good, generous, far above ourselves in many ways. But a time comes when people will grow confidential, —and this has been my experience as a priest; the mask will be lifted, and they will speak of their hidden sorrow. Then it is that we learn that, in spite of appearances, they are suffering like the rest of mankind. Then we can become very humble before them and they become very great. They bear God's mark upon themselves. They are initiated. They know. They know the one thing that is really worth knowing. They know "what is in man." They are poor.

There is a terrible equality among the sons of men.

When I was young, I used to think that there were people who were always happy, enjoyed special privileges, were always successful, and I wondered why it was that there were other people who were always miserable, always unsuccessful, always crushed.

But, as I grew older, I came to know that we all carry the

same burden, that each one bears a load that is just a little above his strength. Each one groans and sighs beneath a weight that is just a little more than he can carry. He is obliged to acknowledge his poverty. He has need of Another. He has need of all the others to help him to bear it. The burden that we ourselves bear reveals the burden that is borne by everyone else. Our misery is fraternal, it teaches us about others, it introduces us into the great fraternity of the poor.

And this is the reason why the apostle should be poor. Only a poor man can be an apostle. He has learned to recognize and to accept his poverty before God, and he is therefore able to go to others and invite them to accept their own poverty as he has accepted his.

The poor man has found something that is so good that he is able to accept his misfortune, something that is so strong that it is able to support his feebleness. He brings to others a message of salvation and of hope. There is a way to be happy, though poor. There is such a thing as an unhappy man who is happy.

Without this experience, without the realization that we are all profoundly alike, one cannot be an apostle, for one cannot be helpful to others unless they can be made to feel that we share their pain with them.

Wealth isolates, wealth disgusts. If we go to others with our riches, we wound them, we provoke opposition. Everyone becomes tense, hard, and makes a desperate effort to hide and to deny his weakness and misery. Each one wears a mask beneath which he hides his own pain and suffering. It is hard to carry your misery written on your face, and that is why each of us puts on a mask in order to give ourselves the air of strength, self-sufficiency, contentment, and capability. As though we had no need for any person, nor for any thing.

This explains why the apostle must go among his fellow men with every appearance of real poverty, so that others may have the courage to remove their masks when they meet him and learn that it is possible to accept their troubles and to look them squarely in the face, for the apostle has found the way to bear his burden with serenity.

The chief characteristic of an apostle is this profound experience which he has had of his own littleness and also of the great things which God effects through the poverty of His servant. Because of this, he approaches others with an attitude of respect and also of friendliness which enables them to acknowledge their own poverty in his presence.

The apostle travels about the world without protection, open to all, poor and helpless, and yet, everyone feels, when in his presence, that his greatest strength lies in his daring to be without everything.

Please notice! We do not serve God in order to become rich. This is a common temptation. God never gives riches to His poor, and seldom does He cure His sick. God does something much greater than that. He enables the poor, the unfortunate, and the sick to find happiness in their poverty, their misfortune, and their sickness.

Even St. Paul himself asked God to make him rich. "I have a sting in my flesh," he wrote, "an angel of Satan, to buffet me." (Just what he meant by this, we do not know. Some malady, a temptation, a sin, whatever it was, it was something that bothered him very much. Some have thought that he was subject to epileptic fits, which could be a great obstacle to his preaching.) "Three times I begged the Lord to deliver me."

(What he really was saying to God was: "Make me a true apostle, —edifying, eloquent, convincing. Make me virtuous, successful. After all, it is for your sake. I will be able to serve you so much better.")

"But He said to me: 'No! My grace is sufficient for you. For my strength is made perfect in your weakness.'"

And Paul then understood that he would be poor all the rest of his life.

And worse than that! We shall be sinners as long as we live. God wants His apostles so poor that He chooses them from among sinners. With this difference: He makes us happy sinners!

Here I must give some explanation, for I know that you are somewhat astonished at my statement.

Yes, there is a beatitude for sinners in Christianity. Happy fault! *Felix culpa!*"

"O God, who has marvellously created the dignity of

human nature and still more marvellously reformed it."
"Much has been forgiven her because she has loved much.
To him who loves less, less is forgiven."

But, understand me correctly. I am not advising you to
commit more sins, I am not encouraging you to increase
your provision, your assortment of sins. I assure you that
you have your full share, and that you need envy no one. If
you could but realize your great lack of faith, hope, and love.
The saints understood this so well that the more they ad-
vanced in holiness, the more they discovered their own sin-
fulness.

In heaven, only pardoned sinners have found entry. (Mary
herself is the first among the redeemed, the humblest witness to the mercy of God.) Those now in heaven are still
marvelling at their pardon. You will never be there until all
your faults become happy faults, faults which recall the
goodness, the tenderness, the joy with which you were
pardoned.

Too often we try to make use of confession itself as a
means of doing without God.

"Confession doesn't do me any good," one will say, "so I
don't go to confession any more." Or another: "It may do me
some good, but not much, because I am always confessing
the same faults."

I see what you mean. You would like to use confession as
a means of doing without confession. You want to make use
of God so that you can do without Him.

But the main purpose of confession is not a means to acquire moral perfection. It is a religious act, it is the occasion of a meeting with the Father, a meeting in which you learn how much He loves you, with what joy and tenderness He pardons you, to what lengths His forgiveness will go, and the wonder of it all.

Hence it is that you still have before you a handsome future of sins, an attractive future of confessions, before you come to know all your weakness, all your ingratitude, and all the mercy of God manifested in that pardon.

If we were not sinners, with more need for pardon than for bread, we would never know the depths of God's love.

Which do you prefer, to be satisfied with yourself, or to be satisfied with God?

You will go to heaven only as poor persons, not because you are content with yourselves, but because you are in admiration of God, happy in being pardoned, astonished at His mercy.

This does not mean that you should always commit the same faults. I believe that when the time comes that you detest your faults less out of pride, when you are willing to be nothing but the opportunity for God to manifest His mercy, in that moment God will grant you a dispensation from sin.

When that time comes, you will know that it is only by His grace that you are preserved, and you will also know that you are always capable of committing sin again. You will feel a fellowship with every sinner, and you will have become capable of assisting them. You will sing with Mary and with all the other "poor sinners" the great things that God can do in the humility of His servants.

But it is much easier to explain all this by looking at the Gospel.

Have you noticed what, in the Gospel, is the very first thing that Christ requires, the first teaching that He gives to His apostles, to those who are to be the foundation of His Church, to those responsible for the Christian fraternity? It is striking. He makes them poor.

No one comes in contact with God without being brought face to face with his own misery. No one has come to know God without, at the same time, coming to know himself, without acknowledging that he is poor and weak and a sinner.

There is only one proof that you have come in contact with a really great person, and that is when you become very small and happy to be so small. If you are satisfied with yourself, proud of your knowledge of your religion, content with your pious practices, virtuous, yet ready to take advantage of every occasion of coming forward, I am certain that you have never met a really great person.

The one proof that you have come in contact with the true God, is that you no longer count for anything. The one proof that you have the true faith is the fear that you have of not living up to it.

Before he met Jesus, Peter was quite pleased with himself. He had great confidence in his natural resources, he knew his own value. His dominating character imposed itself upon others.

But his meeting with the Lord despoiled him of all his self-love. At their very first meeting, the Lord detached him from his natural self-reliance. The Kingdom of God permits entry only to the poor. Peter learned this without delay. The best preparation for the apostolate, for the dignity of supreme head of the Church, was the revelation of his utter incapacity and his innate feebleness. The moment of Peter's conversion was when he cried out, "Withdraw from me, O Lord, for I am a sinful man!" No longer impetuous, no longer sure of himself, no longer ready to take the initiative and carry all the responsibility, Peter was now poor.

It all began on the shore of the lake. This morning the crowd pressed upon Jesus in order to hear Him; and so that He might be heard the better, Jesus stepped into a nearby boat. A little distance away, the men were busy washing their nets. Notice how Christ selects His apostles. He picks them out when they least deserve it. These sermons meant nothing to them. They were busy doing something useful. They had their work to do. And Christ calls them when they least wanted Him.

And it was from Peter's boat that he was teaching the crowd.

Peter himself must have been there, since it was his boat.

He would not have chosen to be present, but since he could not help being there, he listened.

Our Lord was speaking, speaking in a way that Peter had never heard anyone else speak.

Now Peter knew how to appreciate a good speaker, but, after all, listening to sermons was not his real occupation. His business was fishing, and he was a busy fisherman.

And just at that moment, our Lord turned to him and said, "Come, Peter. Let's go fishing."

Peter was taken by surprise. "No use," he said. "I've been over the whole lake. I know, I've had years of experience. We fished all last night and didn't catch a thing." "Let's go anyway," Jesus told him, and then occurred the miracle by which Peter was completely overcome.

Right there, in Peter's own domain, in his own field (if I may use such a word in regard to a lake), Jesus took him down, showed him that, just where he considered himself of great worth, he was worth nothing. Jesus showed him that, without the help of God, he could not catch even one fish.

Peter was converted, but not by a sermon (rare occurrence, that!), but by a fishing expedition, which showed him that he had need of God, even to catch fish.

Perhaps you know someone who says, "It's useless. I can't do anything with the members of my family. I know them too well. It's hopeless. In my neighborhood, in my office, at my work, no apostolate is possible." Or perhaps: "It's useless to try to do anything with me."

And our Lord tells us, "If you will only cast the net once more, not because you have any confidence in yourself, but because you have confidence in me."

Christ made Peter the head of His Church, not because of his worth or his personal ability, but because of his obedience. "At your word, I will cast the net."

And Peter became so convinced of his poverty that he begged the Lord: "Withdraw from me!" He foresaw what it would be like to work with One whose "thoughts are not like our thoughts," and whose power is so out of proportion to our own. Peter understood that his apostolate would mean the abandonment of his independence and his tranquility, the unceasing confrontation of his own nothingness, his own personal insufficiency, and that he would henceforth be subject to the immensity of the designs and the power of God. And he cried out, "Leave me alone! I cannot bear the burden of working with you! I cannot agree to be but the place, the instrument, the occasion, the means by which you will work prodigies out of my misery!"

For his consolation, Jesus tells him only this: "You have seen nothing yet! You have been here catching fish. But soon you will be catching men! Then you will learn what men are and you will long to get away, to withdraw. Only your faith will enable you to persevere. You will have to support not only your own burden but also that of others. You will have to learn to cast your net in the darkness of the night many times and catch nothing."

Then, some day, God's grace comes to us fishers, and we do not know what to do with all those souls that God sends to us.

However, Peter required more than one lesson.

Read the Gospel. Recall Peter's confession at Caesarea: "You are the Christ, the Son of the living God!"

"Ah! How magnificent of you, Peter! But you do not say that of yourself. It is my Father who has revealed it to you."

But, in the next breath, when Christ predicts His coming Passion, Peter comes out with something all his own: "God forbid! Such a thing will never happen!" and he receives the most severe rebuke recorded in the Gospel: "Get behind me, Satan! You do not know the things of God, but only those of men!"

When Jesus foretells the abandonment of his disciples, Peter comes forward again, and draws upon himself the prediction of his own triple denial. But at the time of his final vocation, after his sin and his tears, Peter, now trained, becomes a good fisher of men, —he has become poor. Jesus attempts to arouse his presumption when He asks him, "Do you love me more than these others?" But now Peter does not fall into this trap, this allusion to his "even though all should abandon you, I will not!" His preference for himself is gone, he no longer compares himself with others. And when, for the third time, our Lord asks him, "Peter, do you love me?", Peter is so empty of self, so cured of his pride and his self-assurance, that he has recourse to the omniscience of

Christ and not to his own statement: "Lord, you know all things. You know that I love you."

Thus he is ready to be a good leader, and a true apostle. It would have been terrible to have at the head of the Church one who believed himself chosen because of his own merits.

Instead, we were given a leader who was chosen because of his sin, selected because of his greatest shame.

God desires us to be apostles who know ourselves to be poor. You recall the verse of the psalm: "He has chosen the poor from the dung hill." We would much prefer, in order to be chosen by God, to climb up on some pedestal, but God seeks His apostles, according to the psalm, in the trash heaps, among the refuse, among sinners.

Then the apostle will bear God's message, not because of his own ability, his own virtues, his own merits, —that would repel men. Such wealth would be an insult to their poverty, —but because of his redemption. I would laugh at an apostle who was full of strength and courage, in good health and naturally generous and pure.

But if you have one whose weakness is strengthened by God, a restless person whose restlessness has been stilled by God, an avaricious person whom God has liberated from his possessions, a malicious person whom God has pardoned, then that person has something to say to the world, a message to transmit to everyone; and since we all share the same misery, we may each hope for a like cure, in looking upon him.

It is impossible to pass on to others your good qualities.

They belong entirely to you, and that causes humiliation to others. Only God is communicable. And we must not give souls anything less than Him. If you are a living witness to others of the great things that God has been able to do in your nothingness; if, while longing to go away, you nevertheless remain; and if, while feeling yourself incapable and at the end of your resources, you still hold on, —then you will be able to give to others something far better than yourself: you can give them Him whom you have found.

The whole Gospel says just this. St. Paul was elected when he was poorest. He looked upon himself as a zealous apostle of the Law. But he was guided by his own spirit. He was rich, sure of his teaching, his traditions, his way of life. He wanted to impose them upon everyone, to enchain them, to imprison them, to lead the followers of Christ by force to his own religion, his church, to Jerusalem. There are people today who regard the apostolate like this, —to enslave people, to impose their own ideas, and to keep statistics of their successes and their conquests.

What did God do? What could He do for Paul? He threw him to the earth, down into the dust. When Paul came in contact with the God whom he thought he was serving, he did not recognize Him. He heard a voice which said, "I am Jesus whom you are persecuting."

And if our hearing were better, I am sure we would hear the very same message: "I am Jesus whom you are persecuting."

An examination of conscience will not do. Our consciences

have become so twisted, so subjected to violence, so glossed over, that we must first make an examination of our sub-consciences.

This is what Jesus did to St. Paul, a real psychoanalysis. "Saul, Saul, it is not good for you to kick against the goad."

And Paul then learned that, all the time that he believed that he was serving God, he was really resisting Him. He kicked. He stifled a soft, gentle voice that murmured, "Saul, Saul, why are you persecuting me?" This experience taught him what was in man. His apparent zeal, his apparent good faith, both masked an abyss of refusal given to God, and a like amount of delight in himself. The thing that made Paul an apostle was the experience of his very real poverty. He confessed to Christ, "Who are you? I do not know you. What do you want me to do?" The confession of a poor man.

A fine thing, this, for a doctor in theology to acknowledge that he does not know the God about whom he has lectured so much! And this happens also to some preachers who talk so much about God that they forget to listen to Him. And it is the same with some hearers. They become so accustomed to hearing God spoken of, that they never speak to Him themselves. And with ordinary Christians, too. They have believed for such a long time that they have ceased to believe. They have prayed for so long that now they no longer pray. The habit of not believing has gradually slipped into a too easy habit of believing, and a strong habit of not praying has quietly insinuated itself into a habit of praying too much.

What, then, is to be done?

To become poor! To say, "Have pity on me, O Lord, for I am a sinner!" "Who are you, Lord? I do not know you. Reveal yourself to me. Help my unbelief!"

And Christ will reply to you, "I am Jesus whom you are persecuting. Cease to resist me."

And if we think that we are going to receive any other message, any other vision, than that granted to St. Paul, it is because we are not poor.

Let us listen to Jesus who says to us, "Why do you persecute me? Why do you resist me like this? Why are you always kicking? That is not right, and it does not do you any good to resist me, to refuse me, to close up and become hardened like that, and it makes me suffer besides."

In conclusion, let us take the case of a woman, —the Samaritan.

Christ was poor. So He begins by asking a service of her. "Give me a drink," He said to her, —and He says the same to each of us.

To give is the act of a rich person. The act of the poor is to receive. You are poor if you know how to receive.

The best definition that I have ever heard of a poor person is this: one with whom everybody feels at ease. Quite right, he knows how to receive. People come to his home willingly because they know that it gives him pleasure. You speak to him willingly because he listens so well, that you can tell him things that you would never say to another, things which you hardly dare to say even to yourself. He knows how to receive.

Are people at their ease with you? Do they feel at ease in your community? Do you know how to listen to others? Do others like to speak to you? When Solomon asked wisdom of God, God gave him "an understanding heart," a heart which listens. If you listen well, if you know how to "receive," every one about you will not only have the impression, but also the experience, of bringing something to you, of having something to teach you, and the joy of giving to you.

Christ approached the Samaritan woman by asking for a drink. The surest sign that you are Christ-like, when you visit the sick, the poor, the unfortunate, is that the person whom you have visited will have the impression, upon your departure, that he has given you something; and you also will feel that you have been enriched by your contact with him.

But the Samaritan woman resisted Him. It is not an easy thing to engage immediately in true dialogue, to allow the questioner to enter into one's deepest thoughts and feelings. So she began by being flippant. "How is it," she asked, "that you, being a Jew, are asking a drink of me, a Samaritan?"

Then our Lord tries to make her more serious. "If you knew the gift of God and who it is who says to you 'Give Me a drink,' you would have asked of Him and He would have given you living water."

But she continues her banter, the behavior of those who do not wish to have any contact with you. "Who do you think you are? Do you pretend to be greater than our father Jacob? You don't even have a bucket to draw the water with!"

Jesus tried again but it was useless. There was nothing left to do but to direct the conversation to the subject of her poverty, to her sin. "Go and find your husband."

At that she became sober and answered seriously: "I have no husband."

"You have had five. And he whom you now have is not your husband. Now you are speaking the truth."

"Lord, I see that you are a prophet."

This time He has struck home. She is reduced to the level of her sin. Christ had to bring her down, let her sink, as He let Peter sink when he had set out to have a little promenade on the water. He let him get wet in order that he might learn that it is only when one's hand is in the hand of Christ that one walks upon the water.

After her conversion, the Samaritan woman becomes an apostle. Christ made her poor, spiritually poor at first, and then materially so. She forgot to take her pitcher! Only a poor man can become a missionary.

She went off to find the people of the village and to make the most beautiful declaration of poverty to be found in the Gospel: "Come and see a man who has told me all that I have done!"

All that she had done! How well they knew it! And how tempted they were to make fun of her!

But our Lord had pardoned her so completely that she no longer felt that bitter and sterile shame for her sins. She was too taken up with the marvel of His goodness, His love, the respect and the joy with which she had been pardoned.

She has continued ever since to say to all, "Come and see! There is such a thing as pardon for sin. God alone can remit sins like this. He has made all my faults truly happy faults which remind me only of the mercy, the tenderness, and the joy which He has shown me because of them."

Is it thus that you exercise your apostolate? Is this the message that you are giving to the world? Is this the level at which you pay homage to Him? "There is One who has told me all that I have done. . . . One who has freed me from all my sins. I have never been as happy as this in all my life. He has made of all my faults 'happy faults.' He has taught me to love much because He has pardoned me much. I have come in contact with God and I have learned that, before Him, I am poor, weak, little, and a sinner. But He has made me happy to be poor, weak, little, and a sinner! Come and see what He is able to do for you!"

And she has added the second word of the poor: "Is He not the Christ?"

She knew it. She was sure of it. But she did not say this in order to take advantage over others. What she said was: "Come and try for yourselves. No one has ever spoken to me like this man has. Perhaps He will treat you as He treated me. He said but a word to me and my soul was cured."

Have you a like message to bring to the world? Is it at the level of your blessed poverty that you have become an apostle? Can you invite others to recognize and to accept their own poverty because you have found happiness in yours?

A message like this concerns everyone, and all will come to see it. Not the riches of pride, not a biting sarcasm, but the commonplace fraternity of poverty: "He has told me everything that I have done."

III.

In this chapter we shall meditate on the Gospel and brotherhood. We are going to hear the beating of the heart of the Gospel, because it is the heart of the Gospel which reveals to us that we all have the same Father, that we are all brothers and sisters. For the Christian life is a fraternal life. Yesterday, some of us were speaking of the introduction to the Gospels, and the remark was made that it was as a member of this Fraternity* that he had begun to understand and to relish the Gospel.

In fact, what better introduction to the Gospel could there be than to find oneself surrounded by brethren? Generally, men draw attention to their miserable differences. "I am rich. That man is poor. I have an education. He has none. I am intelligent. He is a fool. I have good health, learning, a good family," and so on, and we forget our chief point of resemblance, —that we belong to Christ. We are incorporated in Christ. He belongs to Christ and so do I. That which is most vital in me is that which comes from Christ. The only thing that will live forever is that in me which comes

---

* La Fraternité catholique des malades et infirmes, N. D. de Bury, to whom this conference was given.

from Christ. "May the Body of Christ keep your soul unto life everlasting."

Thus all that we have that is best, that we hold in common, we have received from Him. We are those poor people whom Christ has put in possession of the most marvellous reality. He has said to us, "When you pray, say 'Father.'" And thus counselled, formed by the divine teaching of our Saviour, instructed by Him, we employ the possessive and say "Our Father." We have claims upon Him. He belongs to us. "Father, I know that you hear me always." "Father, all that is yours is mine." And, thanks to this, all that belongs to me, I can give to you. For what do you have that you have not given to me? So it is that I have learned to give and to love in my turn. God has taught me to love and to give as He loves me and gives to me.

Let us read all this in the Gospels.

When one asks Christians whose religious education has not gone very far, what is the new commandment given by Christ, what is His great commandment, one usually gets this answer: "Love one another." Very well, but if I insist and ask what is new about this commandment? In the Old Testament it is said, "Thou shalt love thy neighbor as thyself." And when Christ was asked which was the greatest commandment of the Law, He quoted from the Old Testament. "When the Pharisees heard that He had silenced the Sadducees, they came together. And one of them, a lawyer, asked Him a question to test Him. 'Teacher, which is the great commandment in the Law?' And He said to him 'You shall love the Lord your God with all your heart, and with all your soul, and with all your mind. This is the great and first commandment. And a second is like it, You shall love your neighbor as yourself. On these two commandments depend all the law and the prophets.'" (Mt. 22, 34–40)

Then, in what way is the commandment of Our Lord new? It is new in this little word that one scarcely notices. The second commandment is the same as the first. It is equal to it, but this presupposes the Incarnation, which means that God has been made man and that He remains so. This means that the Incarnation of Jesus, of the Word, in an individual human nature is merely the prelude to His incarnation in all humanity. Henceforth God lives in every man and waits there to become divine, there to be loved, and there to increase. "He enlightens every man who comes into this world."

In the short space of thirty-three years, Christ was not able to give expression to all the charity which animated Him, nor to all the love for God and for man of which He was the living expression. He could not be sick. He could not be infirm. He could not be the father of a family. He could not know of old age, nor be a leper. He could not suffer abandonment in His old age. And yet, He loved enough to endure all these painful situations. Hence, He now asks of us, who are, so to speak, His "super-added humanity," to enable Him to live over again that human life which He so loved, and through which He so greatly honored the Father, and became the servant of men, —aiding, instructing, encouraging, consoling, curing. Christ has now but one desire, and it is that each one of us should lend ourselves to Him so that He may live again. He would like to have no matter what kind of face, what kind of condition, what kind of family, what kind of life, so that He might fill it with love. He believes that He can save the world by simply living with much love. He wants your life. He would like to live it with you. He would like you to let Him come and live your life, because He believes that He could live it with enough love to accomplish the salvation of the whole world.

The great truth, the great commandment, the great novelty of the Gospel is that fraternal charity has become theological. It is that our neighbor has become God at our doorstep, to receive our love. It makes it possible for us to know whether our love for God is sincere and active, or merely a sentimental dream, —the difference between devotedness, and "devotion."

In Christianity, the love of neighbor takes priority over the love of God. "If you are offering your gift at the altar, and you remember that your brother has something against you, leave your gift there, abandon the altar, and go first to the true God, be reconciled to your brother, and then come and express your love by bringing your gift to the altar."

For the love of God is full of illusions. We imagine God. Or we invent Him. And often we represent Him according to our own image and likeness, or else to suit our convenience. We bring Him near, if need be, or we place Him off in the distance, as is done by changing the focus of a camera. And God is silent. He lets us do as we wish. He effaces Himself. But our neighbor does not let us treat him as we please. He is not silent. Or, if he is, this neighbor of mine, or my father, my mother, my brother, my sister, my wife, my husband, —if he, or she, is silent, there is an attitude far more eloquent than speech. With him, or with her, we always know exactly where we stand.

Christ has promised that the world would be converted, not if we love God, mind you, for anybody can say that and nobody can verify it; but we would today produce that rarest of miracles, that most authentic miracle, if we would begin today to love one another.

As you well know, it is a great joy to any father to see that his children love one another. Every Sunday, when I see my poor Sunday crowd, I say to myself that our Father in heaven must think, when He looks down upon them, "They are a complete failure. My greatest desire is that my children should love one another." — "That they may be *one*, and that the world may believe that you sent me." —That they should love each other, that they should be united to each other . . . And there they are, thinking to please me every Sunday by coming to me as individuals. They never look at one another, they never smile at one another, they never greet one another.

It is the great Christian truth that you are no nearer to

God than you are to your neighbor. How do you stand with your neighbor? Your neighbor at work? Your neighbor on the street? Do you know each other? Do you greet each other? Do you visit each other? Do they come to seek your counsel? When they have need of some service, do they come to you? Are your neighbors at ease in your home? Do they like to come there? Are they well received? Do they like to see you? How do you stand with your neighbor at mass? You are no nearer to God than you are to your neighbor, because God is your neighbor, within the reach of your hand, within the reach of your love. This is what St. Matthew teaches us in his famous passage on the Last Judgment.

This Last Judgment scene begins like something celestial, sentimental, idealistic, and then, all of a sudden, it becomes quite realistic. God has become incarnate. And here is where you feel the shock of the Incarnation.

"When the Son of man comes in his glory, and all the angels with him, then he will sit on his glorious throne. Before him will be gathered all the nations, and he will separate them one from another as a shepherd separates the sheep from the goats, and he will place the sheep at his right hand, but the goats at the left. Then the King will say to those at his right hand, 'Come, O blessed of my Father, inherit the kingdom prepared for you from the foundation of the world; for I was hungry and you gave me food . . .' "

Among the apparitions of the Risen Christ, we have

Magdalen taking Him for the gardener and the apostles taking Him for a cook. He made a fire and on it were cooking bread and fish. This is an apparition of the Risen Christ and a manifestation of the love of the Risen Christ. He cooked them a good meal. When a woman asks herself, "What shall I prepare for dinner today?", what she is really saying is: "How am I going to show them today that I love them?" And so the Risen Christ has shown His love by preparing a good meal for His apostles who had worked hard all the night long and caught nothing.

"I was thirsty and you gave me drink, I was a stranger and you welcomed me, I was naked and you clothed me, I was sick and you visited me, I was in prison and you came to me."

Then the just will reply, "Lord, when did we see you hungry, and we gave you to eat? Thirsty, and we gave you drink? When were you homeless and we took you in? Naked, and we clothed you? In prison, and we visited you?" And the King will anwer them, "As often as You did it to one of my brothers, you did it to me."

To those who are on His left, He says just the contrary. And they are all astonished. "When did we see you?" This is a terrible thing to hear because it is a sort of prophecy that religious teaching will always be faulty. It seems to foretell that it will not be until the Judgment Day that the just and the unjust, both, will understand the Incarnation. Not until then will they comprehend that God was made man and

that He remains so. Not until then will they learn that the
first commandment is the second one, that God has ever
been their neighbor. Let us make a little haste and not wait
until that moment to understand this. It is in the Gospel.
The just, as well as the unjust, are alike astonished at this
judgment. They have never known the Incarnation.

The Incarnation is a difficult thing to accept. Look, for a
moment, at the Eucharist. . . ; every one wishes to partake
of God, to communicate with Him, but do you communicate
with your brothers? When I receive the Lord, I should receive Him with all those who accompany Him, with all
those who are incorporated in Him, with all mankind. Useless to insist, "That person, I cannot bear the taste of him;
that other, I cannot swallow him; and that one, I cannot
digest him." Then you had better not communicate. Your
host will remain in your stomach because you cannot separate the Lord from your brothers, from all those whom He
loves. You must swallow all your brothers with the host of
your communion. You cannot separate Christ from His
Body.

St. Augustine, who was a good popular preacher, said to
his people in Hippo, "It is a very strange thing. If I step on
your foot, it is your tongue which cries out. I did not do a
thing to your tongue. I stepped on your foot."

So it will be on the last day, the head will reproach us for
what we have done to the feet.

And don't imagine that the body of Christ is some sort of

giraffe, with its head up in the clouds and its feet down on earth. His whole body is constantly with us. "I am with you all days." The light shines in the darkness. The Word was made flesh for us, and dwells amongst us. Our religion is not that of the absence of God, but of His presence amongst us, His real presence. Even today He speaks and He feeds us.

The first time that it was said to us: "You are no nearer to God than you are to your neighbor," it was something of a shock. "Oh! But I am sure that I am very near to God, because I so long to possess Him. He gives me such consolation. I feel so good when I am alone with Him. I am so glad that I do not have to occupy myself with others! I fly to Him in order to forget that I am so misunderstood."

God can give you only one consolation, and that is so to penetrate you, so to fill you with His love, that you must return to others again, and become capable of loving them. That is the kind of consolation that God gives. He makes you capable of wanting to love the whole world.

But soon, this statement which, at first, shocked us, becomes something beneficial. If I am no nearer to God than I am to my neighbor, then I am as near to God as I am to my neighbor. Consequently, all that I would do for God, I can do for him. All that I would do, I can do it to my neighbor. I wish to smile at God, then let me smile at my neighbor. I can give God something to eat and drink. I can comfort God. I can pay a visit to God. I can write Him a letter. I can set a nice table. I can cook a nice meal. And for God! What joy! All that I regret that I could not do for God (like Magdalen, Veronica, Simon the Cyrenean), that I can do for my neighbor. And, on the Last Day, He will say to me, "You smiled at me, you visited me, you took care of me. You set the table for me with love, you did the washing for me with love. You cooked good meals for me with love—and one can taste that when one eats, I assure you, —you have lived with me with love." Like the Blessed Virgin. During thirty years, she had to believe that she had in her little house something sacred, something religious, something divine. She knew how to treat with confidence, with respect, with love, that divine something, and, thanks to her, He was able to grow, to become great, to open out and to save the world.

In your own little homes have you enough faith, enough love, so that something divine, something sacred, may grow, may increase, and, one day, save the world? The Blessed Virgin did nothing else but believe that, in the presence of the most ordinary thing in the world, a little child playing about the house, God was present, and by her loving care of that little One, God would become still greater.

And what does it mean, to love one's brothers? In this matter we must not have any false ideas. It does not mean merely to help, to render service, to give. No, to love means to love. God has not said, "Help one another, support one another, be of service to one another." He has said, "Love one another." It means to love him with one's heart, it means to attain to love.

But how can one love others? It seems impossible. "If you only knew!", they will tell me. "It's easy for you to talk. You aren't married, you live alone. If you only knew my wife! my husband! my parents! my children! my neighbors! — then you wouldn't talk like this!"

What is it to love? To love a person is to hope for the best in him always. To love a person means never to judge him. To judge a person means to identify him with something one knows about him. "Now I can pass judgment upon you because I know what you are!" When you do that, you kill him. To love a person is always to expect from him something better.

If I read the Gospel rightly, it seems to me that, from the way Our Lord met people, loved them, drew them to Himself, He always regarded them as children, children not yet grown up, children who have not known enough love. He never identified them with what they had done previously. Take Mary Magdalen, for instance. He expected of her what no one as yet could discover in her. He loved her so much, and pardoned her so absolutely, that He drew from her the purest love, the most faithful love anyone could give. The astonished world about her exclaimed, "Is she really like that? We thought we knew her. We judged and condemned her, and all the while she was like that because she had never been loved enough!" Christ loved her enough to make of her what others, too poor, too mistrustful, too avaricious of their love, could never do.

He went to the house of Zacchaeus, a hated, detested pub-

73

lican. Everyone was indignant and cried out that He was going to eat with sinners. But from what heart among those just men could He have drawn so much faith and generosity? "Lord, behold, I give the half of my goods to the poor, and if I have wronged anyone I restore him fourfold." — "Salvation has come to this house. He is a true son of Abraham."

Christ came upon him at the age when he had stopped growing, no further development was possible because he was not loved enough. Only love causes growth. Think for a moment what a prodigious thing the birth of a human being is. Two adults, fully developed, are going to submit themselves entirely to a little being who does not exist as yet, who has, as yet, no value whatever. But he will be of infinite value in their eyes. They will be ready to sacrifice everything for him, —their time, their health, their money, their lives if need be. And, thanks to such unheard-of prodigality of faith and of hope, the child grows, and awakens one day to meet the smile of that love which has brought him into existence.

When children reach the age of 15, 16, or 17, it often happens that their parents no longer love them. At that age, they feel that they know all about them, and when you feel that you know a person, you no longer love him. "Now I know you, now I can see what you are worth. I will never forget what you have said to me. Now I know what you think of us." They no longer love their children, for to love is to expect great things of them always. When parents cease to credit the all but infinite possibilities that lie dormant in the hearts of their children, then they no longer love them. Then the child stops growing and he feels the need of some friend, —and it does not always matter whom—some friend who will believe in him, and who will expect much of him, and whose love will enable him to continue his development. One strives only for those who give us their love.

Recall when you were young and still living at home. When you returned from a retreat, in which, by accident perhaps, you made a few good resolutions, you began to set the table, or render some other service, and everybody began to make fun of you. "She is converted! He has just come out of retreat. That will all be over in a day or two!" And with their mockery, they ended your efforts to improve. When no one believes in you, when no one expects anything from you, you can no longer improve. And that is why you were always a much better person when you were away from home. Felicitations came to your mother regarding you when you were among strangers, and all because, among them, you felt that they believed in you, they expected the best of you; while at home, all effort was stifled by your unfavorable judgment of one another, by the fact that you no longer expected anything good of each other. Notice the way in which you destroy one another, —by your unkind judgment of one another.

Now think! Suppose, when you were twenty, someone

said to you, "Tomorrow I am going to pass judgment on you. I am going to put down all the good that you have done and, on another page, all the bad that you have done, and you shall be your own judge." What would you have replied? "That's right, I have done those things, but I have not yet shown what capacities I possess. I have scarcely begun to live. No one knows my full potential. I am just waiting for an opportunity to show what I can do." Suppose that this happened at the age of thirty. "You are going to be judged. I am going to see just what you are worth. This is what you have done; this is what you have not done; this is what you deserve." — "Oh yes, it is true that I have acted like this, but the right moment, the right person, the right occasion has not yet come where I can be my real, true self."

You will still be saying the same thing at the age of fifty, and even sixty. An ancient patriarch, at the good old age of 720 years, said this: "The days of my life have been short and evil." He had not had the time to show what was in him because he had not yet found a society which believed in him, hoped in him, and in the midst of which he would have dared to show himself as good as he longed to be.

What is society, fraternity? It is an association where one is more than oneself, thanks to the others, where one has need of others in order to be oneself. You must understand this. Because there are others who expect something of you, who believe in you, hope in you, you become bold enough to be as good, as tender, as humble, simple, obliging, and generous as their approval has encouraged you to be.

76

Do you realize that, in God, there is fraternity? In God, there is need of plurality in order to be God. You understand that. As long as God has been God, He has been a father. God is love. He would not have been love, nor father, all by Himself. He is also Son, and no one is a son all by himself. He is also the Spirit of exchange, and no one can be that, either, all by himself. In God, for Him to be God, there must be others. To be Love, there must be others. And every Sunday, at the Preface, you say to God: "It is truly right and just, proper and helpful towards salvation, that we always and everywhere give thanks to you, O Lord," because you subsist, not in the solitude of a single Person, but in the sharing of the same substance, because you subsist in a fraternity, in an exchange, in love in three persons who are completely transparent in regard to one another, so well do they know and love one another. —Lord, we thank you that you are not a dreadful celibate. Lord, we thank you that you are not a solitary! Lord, how fortunate that you are Love! How fortunate that you are several! How fortunate that you are the noblest, the most beautiful image of what we would like to become!

In God, each person is more Himself in the other persons. Each time that the Father manifests Himself, He says, "Look upon my beloved Son. Hear him. It is in Him that I have placed all that I have. In Him I am well pleased!"

And the Son says, "I do nothing of myself. I say nothing of myself. I do always the things that please Him. He that sees Me, sees the Father also."

And in regard to the Holy Spirit, He says, "He will not speak on His own authority. He will glorify me."

They are lost in admiration of one another.

Have you need of being more than one in order to be yourself? When do you feel most yourself? When you are alone, to think over your hurts? To ruminate your mistakes? Or is it when you have found a fraternity, a group of friends with whom you can be much more your true self when you come together? Friends who love you so well, who have such confidence in you that, when you are with them, you dare to show yourself to be as good, as gentle, as generous, and as gay as it is possible for you to be? And all this you will never be, when you are in the company of those who have no confidence in you.

To love a person means to have confidence in him always. In the Gospel, we see that Christ did this constantly. To the adulterous woman He said, "Go and sin no more!" Thomas He took into His arms. Thomas, the unbeliever, the doubter, violent, obstinent, He placed him within His heart. "Come, Thomas, put your finger into my hands, put your hand into my side, and be no longer faithless, but believing." And Thomas placed his finger in those shining wounds. There he encountered the living outline of the nails, the living expression of the love by which he, Thomas, had been loved. The marvel of being loved like that! He was on his knees, making the most beautiful act of faith in the entire Gospel: "My Lord and my God!" Never before had anyone said anything like that.

Christ expected, awaited, everything from everyone. There sprang up around Him vocations, friendships, such acts of generosity that those who thought they had known these people were taken by surprise. "What! Zacchaeus has become generous? Mary Magdalen has become pure and faithful? Thomas has become a believer? Matthew, the publican, has become an apostle? And all these poor ones, these sinners, are now become apostles? How is it possible?"

Someone loved them. Someone believed in them. Someone did not say, as we often do, "There is nothing to be done with So-and-So. You will get nowhere. I have tried everything. I don't want to see him any more. I no longer write to him. It's just a waste of time."

And Christ goes to each of them saying, "It is because he has never been loved enough that he has become so bad. If he were loved more, he would be a better man. If others had more tenderness, more generosity, more affection for him, he would give up that armor, that hard shell, which he surrounds himself with in order to lessen his suffering."

Rilke, the German poet, says something like this: "There is more truth than one thinks in those legends in which beautiful princesses are changed into frightful dragons, to remain so until a fearless, saintly knight should come along, attack the dragon, and the princess become herself again."

Many of those round about us have enclosed themselves in armor, have transformed themselves into dragons, seem to be bad, churlish, self-sufficient, independent, to need nothing and no one, and they are dying of fear and of loneliness in the fortresses which they have built around themselves. Many of these terrifying people are nothing but poor, helpless beings who are waiting for someone to come to their assistance. All that is needed is that some fearless soul approach them with much love and confidence, with sweetness and patience, in order to deliver them from themselves, to free them from the armor plate which they have covered themselves with in order to protect themselves from suffering, but which, at the same time, keeps out life and love.

Let us believe with our whole soul that God dwells in each one of His creatures, and that He there waits to be sought out, to be set free, so that He may expand and carry out His divine purposes.

I believe that our world wants nothing so much as to be converted. I do not say that as a pleasantry. Ours is a magnificent epoch, but it is also serious, and also tragic. Do you study, do you love, the age in which you are living? There is no way of loving God without loving the world. You cannot believe in God without believing in the world. If you love God, you love also the world. The one and only proof of your love for God is your love for your brethren. St. John tells us that the sign by which we have passed from death to life is that we love our brethren. To be passionately in love with God is to be passionately in love with the world, because the God whom you so love lives in the world. Each morning He sends His son, His daughter—you—into the world to save it.

God believes in the salvation of the world, God hopes for the salvation of the world. He loves it, and you cannot love Him without loving the world.

Do you recall this passage from the Gospel? "Christ said to the crowds, 'When you see clouds at sunset, you immediately say, It is going to rain, and it does rain. And when you notice that the wind is blowing from the south, you say, It will be warm, and that is what happens. Hypocrites! You know how to read the signs on the earth and in the sky, but you cannot read the signs of the time in which you are living.'"

Do you study the signs of the time? I think, in considering the signs of our time, that this is very evident. The world is looking for truth. It does not believe, and it suffers from its disbelief. And to suffer from a lack of faith is the beginning of having faith. It does not hope, but it suffers because it is unable to hope. It does not love, but when one suffers because one does not love, that is the beginning of love.

Our world asks for nothing so much as its own conversion, but it will never be converted to God unless it finds a true Church, a true Fraternity. Our world is too realistic to yield to reasoning, demonstrations, and Scholastic proofs. Like St. Thomas, it wants to see and to touch. It wants to find hands that are open, hearts that are open, a reception that is affectionate and trustful.

Out of the Church, no salvation! The world will never believe in God until it sees a true Church. The world will

81

not believe in the Resurrection of Christ if you lead it to the public library there to study the sources of Christianity. To the world, there is only one proof that Christ is risen and that He is living, that His love is still living in the world, living in your love. The only proof that the love of Christ is living in the world is that you yourself are living in love, which means that you should love others with a love that surpasses the natural resources of your heart.

Out of the Church, no salvation!

"Where two or three are united in my name, that is where I am." There, where two sick persons love each other and are united and look for a third companion, there is where God is. That is where there is fraternity. That is where there is a true Church. And this world of ours, like St. Thomas, wants to feel, to handle, a true Church, and true love. That is what it needs most.

In our days, one observes this striking contrast. There are conversions only among the upper classes. Among the masses, there is apostasy. Do you know why? Because these elite can study, reflect, handle documents, read books, and become convinced that Christianity is the truth, but the mass must be content with looking on, with looking at us, and very often this spectacle does not encourage them to make the sacrifices that a conversion would entail, and with no other result than the advantage of resembling us. The world needs a Church in which the love of the Risen Christ is living, a society in which one is loved, where one is more oneself because there are others, and where one is at home with these others.

The world will not be converted without a miracle. Without miracles, there is no religion, no conversion, no faith. When Christ came, He had His hands full of miracles. He filled the world with miracles. He astonished the world with His miracles.

But, pay attention to this! For a miracle to be efficacious, it should be within the range of the interests of the one who is to benefit by it. Christ had to deal with simple people. They were thirsty, so He changed water into wine. Thus He placed on their table six jars of good wine. That caught their attention, that made an impression. Others were fishermen, so He allowed them to make a miraculous draft of fish—one hundred and fifty-three large fish! Others were hungry, so He multiplied the loaves. Others were sick, and He cured them.

In our day, miracles like this would not be considered as being truly religious events.

If someone today began to change water into wine and to multiply loaves of bread, all he would attract would be a crop of swindlers, and he would be accused of lowering the prices of farm products. In our day, we do not suffer from famine alone, but also from over-production. Thus it is that Christ has something much more important to do than to change stones into bread. He has to change our hearts of stone into hearts of flesh, and work the stupendous miracle of teaching us to share our surplus with those who have too little.

And were anyone to appease tempests or to walk upon the water, I am sure that the government would kidnap him and lock him up in a laboratory to prepare for some future war.

Have you noticed the passage in the Gospel? When Christ walked on the water, or multiplied the loaves, what did the people want to do? He had to flee because they wanted to make Him their king. He would have solved one of the greatest of military problems, that of transportation. He could walk on the water. And the problem of food. He multiplied the bread. The logistic base of military operations is assured. They can now conquer the world. Then Christ fled, disgusted.

The miracle for our time, the miracle that our world needs, (—just as those people needed wine, bread, health, fish,)—the miracle for our day, the miracle which will bring about the conversion of the world, is the miracle of love and fraternity among Christians. "See how they love one another." Our age is cruelly divided by nationalism. By our interdependence upon one another, we have become a single body, like the human body. And when there is the least little eruption in no matter what part of this world, the entire body has a fever. But that body is inhabited by millions of little souls who are frightened, cold, timid, hostile, rebellious, who cannot bring themselves to come together and to love one another. The miracles which Christians have to work is the miracle of their mutual love. Wherever there is a Christian, there should be fraternity. In this is a challenge and a call to love.

It is difficult. One must always expect great things of others but never exact anything. That is the paradox of love. If you require that others change before you will love them, if you wait until they are deserving of it, you will wait a long, long time! And if you leave them as they are, if you hope for nothing of them, if you arouse nothing, then you have loved badly.

You must hope against hope. You must have both attachment and detachment. I have said that we must be happy, even though unhappy, happy though poor, happy though persecuted, and attached though detached. We must expect much and exact nothing.

So then, what the world is waiting for is that you should work this miracle of loving one another. The greatest service that you can render to a fellow being is to set before him a model in which he can see his own possibilities and strive to achieve success. A teacher does that for his students. The greatest help that we can give to our teen-agers is love. They lack so much, the poor things, that they put on masks in order to make a show before the world. Such absurd masks, so idiotic: movie stars, athletic champions, the latest book that they have read, the latest film that they have seen, — horrible masks, sometimes. And the whole work of their educators is to love them enough and respect them enough, to set before them models in which they can see what they can make of themselves and try to become like to it. When you love another, you do that, and you love him so much that, in your presence, he dares to remove his mask and begins to try to be as good, as docile, as generous as you wish him to be, and which he has never dared to be with anyone else, because of the encouragement which you have given him.

Our age also waits for someone to place before it a model in which it can see what it would be like, and strive to attain that goal. Take a look at those models which our modern musicians, our modern painters, our modern sculptors offer to the world. They are often terrible, even tragic. But their art has at least the merit of not being academic, it is not a copy. They try to invent, to make a guess at the model that the world would like to have.

Are we incapable of placing before the world a model of love, of fraternity, in which it can see what can be done and go to do it? The world will be converted when it sees a true Church, where we are united among ourselves and loving one another and offering to it a model in which it will recognize what it has been longing for and has sought in vain in so many other places.

IV.

PERHAPS, having come this far, you are a little tired now, so I will try not to disturb you too much. And in any case, the words of God often come to us when we are drowsy, or asleep. The proof? Look at the Old Testament, and even the New Testament, and see how often the Lord manifested Himself in a dream. In order to find a man somewhat tranquil, a little receptive, God is reduced to the necessity of speaking to him while he sleeps. A proof, too, that agitation is not an exclusively modern phenomenon.

As a matter of fact, we are now going to speak of these communications of God since the subject of our discourse is prayer and brotherhood. My argument will be very simple: there is no true brotherhood without prayer, no true love, if its source is not the heart of God Himself.

There can be no true brotherhood without prayer. It is God who must send us out to our brethren. Don't go of yourself. God loves your brethren far more than you do, and it is God's love that you must bring to them. It is much better than your own.

Why is charity a theological virtue? Because we are so poor that nothing less than God must come into our hearts

so that we may love those we love most in the way in which
they need to be loved. These are our relatives, our neighbors,
our friends. Without God, our love becomes sterile, enervated. True love never uncovers itself, never reveals itself,
until after there has been some experience of one's poverty.
I can read that in the Gospel story of the wedding at Cana.

At Cana, the two spouses were awakened to the realities
of life at the wedding itself, —at the wedding feast. They
had a harrowing experience of poverty, there was no more
wine, no more juice, nothing. Here was a feast that threat-
ened to dissolve in water, and a marriage to go on the rocks.
They were having the unpleasant experience that their re-
serves, their newly pooled resources, were insufficient. Their
disillusionment, their recognition of their predicament, followed, for once, immediately upon their marriage. Fortu-
nately, Christ was there. Someone said a prayer, someone
turned to Him in this joyous fraternity of guests. And there
followed but a gesture, a slight intervention, a miracle from
Christ, and the second wine was better than the first.

In a fraternity, in a family, in a marriage, in a religious
vocation, the second love is the better. The first flush is too
human, too much of flesh and blood, of ambition, of vanity,
of egotism, of reveries, pious though they may be. What is
needed is some disillusionment, a terrible experience though
it can be. One says to oneself, "I feel just about ready to quit
that society. It is not at all what I thought it would be. There
is no enthusiasm there, no warmth, no love at all." A fruitful

experience of poverty, this! It forces one to look beyond the human, to go deeper, and to seek from God that love which one would wish to give to others, —to ask Him to provide the bread that others will come to eat at your table.

We must be nourished by God before we become capable of loving others and making them happy. What we must offer to others is not our questionable character, our hypocrisy, our sternness, —already insupportable even to ourselves. There are those who rush into some apostolic work because they cannot bear to rest quietly before God. They make one think of musicians who are so preoccupied with the concert, so anxious to take part in it, so eager to make noise with all the rest, that they never take the time to tune their instruments. Their playing is horribly false and yet, all the time, they imagine that they are giving great pleasure to others.

Christ has said that He would not entrust Himself to men. He knew what was in man. He has said something shocking: "You who are evil." And worse still: "He who enters not by me is a thief and a robber. They come—[this is a terrible thing to hear when one is an apostle, and I mean myself as well as you]—they come only to steal and slay and destroy." You will say, "Not at all! You exaggerate! I come to do good, to spread the truth." Oh yes, you have come to bring *your* truth, to use it to make yourself a person of importance, to win approbation and success. But, should some one else speak those same truths, you would be uninterested, you would make objections, you would criticize, you would ridicule. All this in order to give the impression that you know much better. It is not truth which is important to you, but your reputation.

Or another will say, "Of course not! I wish to devote myself, I wish to spend my life, I would even give my life, in the service of others." Alas! Just another way of achieving importance! "How is that? Why, I would give my life for So-and-So." Oh yes, but on condition that it is you who save him. If it should happen that he is saved by someone else, you would, possibly, regret his salvation.

Recently, I met a woman who had been praying for the conversion of her husband for the space of thirty years. He came back to the faith through the efforts of someone else. She is still resentful about it. "And who will throw the first stone?"

We are always ready to defend ourselves. How many people get so annoyed with Our Lord that they want to send Him other adorers. They look for replacements.

It is never safe for you to leave the church until you wish you could stay longer. This will undoubtedly mean that your visits will not be short ones.

When you can say with St. Peter, "Lord, it is good to be here. I would like to remain and erect my tent," then you are ready to leave. At that moment, He is sending you out into the world, He, not you. When the one who sends is yourself, then the results are lamentable. You go to steal, to slay, and to destroy. You go to impose yourself upon others, to display your own importance.

All Christianity is a matter of learning how to die and how to rise again. It is to believe that Christ is One to whose death and resurrection we can always unite ourselves.

At baptism, you were drowned, like little kittens, and you emerged, dripping with clean water, renewed, reborn.

Going to confession is like dying and rising from the dead. It could be compared to a suicide, where one gets rid of a troublesome, unbearable person, which one is, to oneself and to others. All that is necessary is to enter the confessional. There one dies to one's self-will, to those poor, sad doings that are one's sins, and yields to the will of God, which is love and tenderness, peace, indulgence, joy.

At Mass, we are united to the death and resurrection of Christ. "Here," you say, "is my life, I have had enough. Take it. Here is my food. I do not want any more. I do not trust it to sustain me. Here is my day. I do not want to live it. Take it." And God gathers up your food, your day, your life. He blesses them, He consecrates them, He transforms them, He transubstantiates them, and then He gives you *His* food, *His* day, and it is He who comes to live *His* life in you.

If you are not dead and risen again, you know nothing of Christ. Before undertaking any apostolate, you will have to kill yourself. How can you bring to others a message of resurrection if you are not dead?

Prayer is, above everything, a unique experience of death and resurrection. You are certainly well aware of it. What is harder than to pray? What is harder than to die?

To pray is to bring death to an area in which we are but

too much alive. One of my Trappist friends said to me, "When you come to prayer, it is impossible to stop your car and get out if your engine is still turning at the same speed." You go to the chapel, you stop your car, but the engine, your anxious, agitated, enervated, tormented, frightened, vindictive mind, is still turning at high speed. You haven't gotten out of the car yet.

Christ took a whole night in which to make one request of His Father: "May your will be done." And we swallow the whole *Pater* at one gulp.

Do you know what you, and most Christians together with you, are saying when you rattle off the "Our Father"? A prayer that is purely pagan. Not being dead, you do not know how to say it. That prayer can be said only by those who have been instructed in the precepts of the Gospel, formed by our dead and risen Lord's divine teaching. When one is not dead, here is the prayer that he says: "Our Father, remain in heaven. As long as you do not mix in my affairs, I shall be in peace. If you do not interfere, all will go well. As long as the direction of events is in my hands, I am confident, but if you take the steering wheel, we shall risk some bad turns. May my name be honored, sanctified, saluted, recognized. May my kingdom come; may my influence spread; may my business prosper; may my good reputation be known far and wide; and, above all else, Lord, may my will be done." —Have you ever prayed for anything else? You will have to be dead, dead to yourself, as Christ

was, in order to say, "May your will be done and not mine."
Prayer is a wonderful experience of death and resurrection. Prayer is transforming. We always begin by asking for
what is not good. One must die to all that one is asking for
and become aware of the One from whom one is asking it.

A mother comes to pray that her child may not die. Everyone has told her that there is no hope. "There is nothing that
we can do." The doctor tries to reason with her, and says,
"We have tried everything." Her husband tries to calm her:
"Accept what the doctor has said." She is angry with the
doctor and she is angry with her husband. She tells them
that even if they all abandon hope for the child, she will not.
Then she goes to pray. She has come to tell God that He
cannot permit such a thing, that she will never forgive Him,
that she does not want her child to die. But, if she prays long
enough, if her prayer is earnest enough, this same thing
happens over and over again. When she leaves, she will be
astonished at the words that she finds herself saying: "I
place my trust in you. I offer my child to you. You will take
better care of him than I ever can, you know far better than
I what is best for him." When she returns to her home, calm,
serene, peaceful, strong, everyone asks, "What is this? What
did she do? Where has she been? What has happened?"

She has prayed, and she has died to a part of herself where
she was but too much alive, —her anxiety, her fear, her
exasperated defiance, —and she has risen in a part of herself
where she was dead: in faith, hope, and trust. She has con-

sented to die to what she was asking, and she has risen to the power and the love of Him from whom she was asking.

When we come to prayer, in the scale of our existence, the dish on God's side of the scale is light, so light that it is lost in the clouds, high up, invisible, weightless, hardly existing at all. And the dish on our side is heavy, weighed down. There are mountains of care, mountains of resentment, mountains of sensuality, mountains of enervation, mountains of disgust, mountains of discouragement. They weigh very heavily on our side of the balance. What are we going to do to reëstablish equilibrium? Change the lever of the scale? Not at all. Change the weight in the dishes. We must fill God's side with much prayer. Very quietly, God becomes a living Being, God comes closer, God becomes good, God becomes God. And then, one hardly knows when, the dish on our side begins to rise. It is true that prayer can move mountains. It is true that the dish that was stuck in the mud has, at some moment, risen from the mire.

My life is supportable if God exists, if God loves me, if God is living. My burden is tolerable, my life bearable. I can be a happy poor person. I can keep going a long time yet, but only if God becomes truly my God.

When there is no prayer in your life, there is no God. You show your esteem for God by the time you allot to Him. If you have no time for God, no matter what your pretexts, no matter what your excuses, you have no esteem for God. Your employment of time is determined by your judgment of values, and if God has no place in your time it means that He has no value. You have time for whatever you consider important, —fix your hair, look after your clothes, read a newspaper, a little conversation with someone, three or four meals a day, for instance. If there is no place for God, it is because He is unimportant. Without prayer, you are practically an atheist.

He who does not pray, does not believe in God. He pretends to believe, he seems to long for God. He says, "Ah! If I could only pray! If I had the time for prayer! How I would love to be a soul of prayer!" They tell me that when a man has been unfaithful to his wife, he feels a longing for her, he finds that she is the best woman in the world, he condemns himself, and, generally, he brings her a gift. When a man brings his wife a gift, I am told, it is because he has done something for which he must seek her pardon. I do not want to upset households, so just let me say that, if you long for God, if you desire to pray, and if you regret that you have not the time, —if you think yourself a contemplative, and yet you do not pray, then you are trying to deceive God.

There is no God in your life if there is no prayer.

For God asks of our time. That is annoying. In order to act upon our lives, God must have time. When we go to prayer, we are so full of ourselves, so agitated and upset by our many cares, that we are not receptive of God. A stomach that is contracted by a spasm cannot digest the food. Trepidation excludes receptivity. Modern physicians attribute many of our ills to the speed with which we live. Calm is necessary and also rest. If you read the Gospel, you will notice with astonishment that Christ always begins by refusing the petitions addressed to Him. This is instructive for us, for does it not correspond to our own experience?

The good, tender, compassionate Christ almost always begins by refusing to do what is asked of Him. Even when His mother told Him that they had no wine. (Do you know any of the forms of prayer given in the Gospel that will help you to pray? The greater number of the faithful are ignorant of prayers, they have nothing to say to God because they have not learned by heart some of the words of God which they might repeat. Go before God and say to Him, "Lord, there is no more wine, —no more faith, no more love, no more energy." Say it with the Blessed Virgin: "There is no more wine.") And Christ begins by a refusal. "What of it? What is that to you and me? My hour is not yet come." What did the Blessed Virgin do then? Did she go away saying, "I am not surprised. I knew it would be that way. One is never heard. He always refuses." Not her! She has even greater confidence. She is calm and even more at the disposal of God. What she said was: "Do whatever He tells you." She had confidence, not in the thing that she had asked for, but in Him of whom she had asked it, and she was heard.

Martha and Mary—and remember, Jesus loved Martha

and Mary—sent word to Him that Lazarus was sick. Another beautiful prayer for those who are not well, a prayer that is so tender, so confident, so discreet. "Lord, he whom you love is sick." Go to the church, sit down and rest a little, then say, "Lord, he whom you love is sick, he is very sick. His faith is sick, his hope is sick, his love is sick, and his confidence is sick, too." That is prayer enough. There are people who want to say all those sublime things like "Lord, I love you above all things. I firmly believe all that You have revealed." Much better to use the words of the Gospel: "Lord, I am blind. Grant that I may see! I am deaf. Grant that I may hear! I am mute; grant that I may speak! I am paralyzed; grant that I may move! I am a leper; purify me! I am dead; bring me back to life. I am sick; cure me!"

Our words must be very simple and they must be truthful. "Help my unbelief!" Those are true prayers. You go before God and you say, "Lord, I am tired. Lord, I warn you that I shall not stay long. If you do not keep me, I shall be gone within two minutes. I am tired already, and I am thinking of the heap of things that I have to do. Grant that I may stay, keep me with you a little while, help me to pray a little, teach me to pray." That is a true prayer. "Lord, he whom you love is sick!"

Christ, having learned that Lazarus was sick, remained where He was another two days. Two days, time enough to die, time enough for them to die to what they had asked. They asked that He would cure Lazarus, and He intended

97

to bring him back from the dead. Christ always begins by refusing in order to open our souls, to dig deep into them, because He wishes to give us much more than we are willing to receive, and because, as St. Paul tells us, in prayer we know not what to ask, so the Holy Spirit Himself asks for us, "with unspeakable groanings."

To pray is to place oneself entirely at the disposition of God so that He may, for once, do for us what He is always wanting to do for us, and which we never leave Him the time, the opportunity, nor the liberty to do. And as He has much to say to us, much to do in us, and much to give, He needs a long time. "Work in me, O Lord, and grant that I may let you work." To pray is an act of faith, it is to believe that God is active and beneficent.

To pray is to expose oneself to God. You all know what it is to expose oneself to the sun. On the beaches, at this very moment, this cult of the sun has recruited innumerable *devotées*. All those people have a blind confidence in the sun. They believe it to be beneficial, curative, beautifying. From time to time they are disappointed. They hope to turn brown and they turn red! They hope to become strong and they come down with pleurisy. Our great-grandmothers protected themselves against the sun in order to have a lily-and-rose complexion. Our conduct is just the opposite, but we follow it with the same faith and the same strictness. For three, four, even five hours a day, there they are, exposed to the sun in order to get tanned. They sacrifice everything, and, three weeks later, it is all gone.

When I see this, I feel very much humiliated. I say to myself, "You could never do for God what these people do for the sun. You have never had the faith in God that they have in the sun. You have never exposed yourself to God for three hours, not for three weeks. Is this because you do not believe that God is more beneficent, more active, more efficacious than the sun?" Do you expose yourselves to God? What is the measure of your faith in God?

The time of prayer is the time of the incarnation of God within ourselves. It is the time when we allow Him to work upon us so that He may transform us into Himself.

Let us follow a little further in the Gospel the debate between God and man, —God wishing to give man more than he is willing to receive. Recall the officer of the king in St. John's Gospel. He learned that Jesus had come from Judah, and he galloped off with his attendants in search of Him. His son is at the point of death and he has but one desire, one last hope: to find Christ and bring Him back with him so that He might cure his son, for he had heard that the touch of the Lord worked wonders. He threw himself at the feet of Christ and begged Him to come and cure his son. Jesus received Him in a manner which astonishes us, —so cold and hard. "Unless you see signs and wonders, you do not believe." The man did not let himself get into a discussion. He prayed, "Come, Lord, before my little one dies." We would have thought that Christ would have yielded, that He would have been touched by this plea. "Go," He tells the officer, "your son lives."

Notice! We understand that to mean that the request was granted, but the officer took it for a refusal. He knew that Christ had cured by contact, and what he wanted was to bring Christ with him to the child and have Him touch the boy. Then he would have been sure of his cure. Christ said to him, "I will not come. You must believe. Go home alone." The man stood there, exhausted, trembling. He had been asked, as usual, for the one thing in the world that cost him most. He saw himself returning to his home, and his wife coming to meet him and asking, "The prophet? You could not find Him?" — "Yes, I found Him." — "And you did not bring Him with you?" — "He would not come." — "Well, then, your child is dead." He waited, not daring to leave, and saying to himself that he had lost the one chance in his life. He did not dare to insist, knowing that that would be a lack of faith. The apostles surrounded him, saying, "If you will only believe! If you will only believe! If you will only have confidence in Him!" And then, after a while, the man turned and left without saying a word. The effort that was asked of him took all his strength. He could say nothing. He went like one almost dead.

The following day—it took a long time for that prayer— he saw his servants coming to meet him. "Your son is living!" — "At what hour did he grow better?" — "Yesterday, at the seventh hour, the fever left him." — "And he recognized that it was at that hour that Christ had said, 'Your son lives,' and he believed and all his household."

Understand: he had come to ask a favor of Christ, to extort a miracle of Him, because he thought Him a thaumaturgus, and Christ refused to be used like that. Christ required his complete confidence, not in what he had asked but in Him of whom he had asked it. Christ does not wish to give anything less than Himself. He will not grant you a favor that you can take away with you and leave Him alone. He desires to begin a friendship with you that will last forever.

To throw further light on this subject, nothing is more beautiful nor more characteristic than the story of the Canaanite woman. She was a pagan, a Syrophenician. She pursued Christ with her cries: "Cure my daughter! Cure my daughter!" He did not answer her a single word. What hardness! You recognize that hardness? How many times has He not answered you a word? How many times has He made you wait? Then the apostles, plain unpolished men as always, said to Christ, "Shut her up! She is breaking our eardrums!" That was the extent of their charitable intervention. And Christ replies, "I was sent only to the lost sheep of the house of Israel." But she kept on shouting even louder: "Cure my daughter!" Christ gives her an even harder answer. "It is not fair to take the children's bread and throw it to the dogs." Now "dog" was the name that the Jews used for strangers. This woman must have been from the south, she is so full of heart, wit, and vivacity. She catches the ball on the bounce and replies, "But, Lord, do not the little dogs

eat the crumbs that fall from the table of the children?"
Then Jesus looked at her and I think He must have smiled.
He said to her, "Woman, great is your faith. Be it done as
you wish."

She, too, in the beginning, wanted to wrench from Christ
a favor, a miracle, and, with it, depart far from Him. Christ
had no intention of taking part in a game like that. He dug
deep into her soul, He desired to have an act of complete,
total, unquestioning faith gush forth from her heart. So He
tested her. He spoke harshly to her. And she allowed herself
to be so tried, she experienced her own poverty. She allowed
Him to despoil her of all her own self-love and nationalism,
and she displayed so much ingenuity, so much confidence,
such a joyous poverty, that she and Christ became friends.
They recognized each other and they smiled at each other.
Between friends, gifts never do any harm. Between strangers, a gift is a dangerous thing. Usually it is not exactly "dis-
interested." Christ knew how to establish between Himself
and this pagan woman a bond that would endure forever, a
friendship that would last throughout eternity.

God does not wish to give anything that is less than Himself. He attaches Himself to that thing which is being asked
of Him and never lets the petitioner get away with only the
thing that he has asked for. Even Christ Himself prayed
like this. He began by asking what He was not to receive.
He began by saying, "If it be possible, let this chalice pass
from me. If it be possible, let this chalice pass from me."

And because He prayed a long time—the whole night—when He rose from His knees, He said, "Not my will, but yours." Be simple enough and humble enough to partake of the weakness of Christ before presuming to partake of His strength. Go to the chapel or the church and stay long enough to repeat: "That shall not be. That shall never be. I cannot accept it. I do not want it, and, if I did want it, I could not endure it. It is useless to ask that of me, I will not give it. And if I should give it, I would be so unhappy that I would become thin and mean. Do not speak to me about that. Choose something else."

You will have to argue a long time with God. You will have to complain long and speak much and then you will discover that, little by little, you are paying more attention to Him to whom you are speaking and less and less to the thing you are speaking about.

Prayer is what makes God become alive to you, and it takes time for Him to grow, it takes time for the words of God to become active. I do not know your method of prayer, but I have noticed that, in the Gospel, there are two contradictory counsels, and I would like to know how you solve the problem. On the one hand we read, "Do not multiply words as the pagans do, who hope to be heard because they speak much. Your heavenly Father Himself knows what you have need of." He knows much better than you do and He loves you.

On the other hand, we are told that we should pray always. Christ prayed entire nights. I wonder what you do? As for myself, I know of only one way and that is to say the same thing over and over. That is the way Christ prayed. "He went away, saying the same words." This was the method used by the Blessed Virgin. "She kept all these words, repeating them in her heart."

It takes a long time to say a thing before we say it truly. Think of Christ: "For He, in the days of His earthly life, with a loud cry and tears [He prayed, He wept, He cried, —you would have been scandalized to see Christ refused, struggling, tormented], offered up supplications to Him who was able to deliver Him from death, and was heard because of His reverent submission. And He, Son though He was, learned obedience from the things that He suffered."

He asked that He might not die, and He received the grace to endure. He was given much more than He had asked. And you, son or daughter that you are, you will learn by your own sufferings what it is to obey, and you will know that you have received far more than you asked.

I believe that every prayer is always heard. I have found this to be the most astonishing and the most instructive thing in the lives of many of the people whom I have known. In the darkest moments of their lives, in time of bereavement, of trial, of suffering, when they were asked, "Are you sure that you never asked this of God? Are you sure that you never made an offering of this to God? Are you sure that you never prayed for this?", they suddenly recognized a prayer of long ago which they never believed would have been so well answered.

God is more attentive than we think to what we ask of Him. He hears us and He is faithful in recovering during the course of our lives that which we once offered Him and have so often taken back since then. Some of life's puzzles become clear when we can say, "I offered that to God. Yes, I said to Him, 'Your will be done, not mine,' but I had forgotten all about it." Then, when some sorrow, or trial, comes, someone reminds us. "This is from God. Don't you remember? You asked for this, you made this offering."

Every prayer is heard because it was first inspired by Christ Himself. It is God who prays in you. It is not you who pray but God who is calling you to make this prayer. When you come to prayer, you ought to begin with shouts of joy, saying, "God is at work within me. God has already worked the miracle of bringing me to my knees, and now, if I remain long enough, if I am attentive enough, I am going to find out that He has already heard me. I am going to learn what He wishes to give me." It is God who wishes to give to us, not we who wish to receive.

The greater number of people never recognize the answers to their prayers during the course of their lives. The New Testament begins with this event. Zachary had always prayed for a child and he never had one. Even at the age of eighty years, he continued to pray. Prayer was his profession.

He was priest, even high priest, and now in a special office. But he prayed without heart. He prayed without faith. He prayed through habit. There is a habit of not praying which insinuates itself into a habit of praying too much. Have you ever experienced that? And when an angel appeared to him to tell him, "Your prayer has been heard. Your prayer has been answered. You will have a son," Zachary replied, "That is impossible. At my age? And the age of my wife? You don't seem to know what you are talking about." And he had to be punished before he would yield.

I can understand Zachary because of my experience with one of my students. He was a fine boy of fourteen, straightforward and unaffected. His father was dying and was a lapsed Catholic. The whole college was praying for his conversion and his recovery. Coming to the college one Sunday evening, he asked to speak to me. "Father," he said, "a priest was at our home this afternoon, a friend of my father. He stayed with him a long time, and, as he was leaving, he said to me, 'Jack, good news! Your father has made his confession: —'Father,' I asked, 'do you mean that he is converted?' — 'Of course, Jack. Your father is an honest man and he would not have gone to confession if he were not converted.'" Then the boy looked at me. "It's funny, Father. I have been praying for this since the time of my First Communion, and now I can't bring myself to believe it."

At the age of seven, he had added a "Hail Mary" to his night prayers for the conversion of his father, and, as usual, he had not been heard in the way and at the time that he expected. So he gave up hope. Of course, he continued his prayer, he would not dare to omit that "Hail Mary" from his night prayers. And when he learned that his prayer had been answered, he was the last person in the whole family who would believe it.

And, nevertheless, his very first prayer had been heard. He prayed because God inspired him to pray. It was the same with Zachary. He was promised an extraordinary child, and it was God who willed that he should pray for that child. When he was not heard at the time, and in the way, that he expected, he did not think that he would ever be heard. Finally, when his prayer was answered, he refused to believe what he was told.

Even the Blessed Virgin. God had inspired her vow of virginity. At that time, she decided to consecrate herself wholly to God, to renounce motherhood, to be poor, and God placed a child in her arms. It was for this that she had consecrated herself to God because the child was God. And the Virgin Mary was the only one who recognized in this extraordinary happening the answer to a prayer. Because she was so poor, God could place His own Son in her arms.

Let us ask the Blessed Virgin to teach us to pray, to admit that this is what we have asked for. That a habit of no longer believing may not insinuate itself into a habit of believing too much; that a habit of not praying may not slip quietly into too routine a prayer. When Christ hears us, as He always does, may we thank Him and recognize our own prayer in the occurrence which now threatens to take away our peace.